Blueprint Crochet

MODERN DESIGNS FOR THE VISUAL CROCHETER

Robyn Chachula

INTERWEAVE
interweavebooks.com

Editor: Katrina Loving

Technical Editor: Julie Holetz

Art Direction and Design: Connie Poole

Photography: Brooks Freehill

Hair & Makeup: Catherine Corona

Special thanks to Prospect New Town, Longmont, Colorado.

Text © 2008 Robyn Chachula

Photography © 2008 Interweave Press LLC

Illustrations © 2008 Interweave Press LLC

Interweave Press LLC

201 East Fourth Street

Loveland, CO 80537-5655 USA

interweavebooks.com

Printed in China by Asia Pacific Offset

Library of Congress Cataloging-in-Publication Data

Chachula, Robyn, 1978-

  Blueprint crochet : modern designs for the visual crocheter / Robyn

Chachula, author.

    p. cm.

Includes index.

ISBN 978-1-59668-072-2 (pbk.)

1. Crocheting--Patterns. I. Title.

TT825.C378 2008

746.43'4041--dc22

               2008008681

10 9 8 7 6 5 4 3 2 1

interweavebooks.com

Acknowledgments

This book is the absolute icing on the cake for me in terms of fulfilling one of my childhood dreams. I did not do it alone, and there are many I would like to thank.

First and foremost, I would like to thank Interweave for taking a gamble on a relatively new but highly excited crochet designer and helping her learn the ropes along the way. To the yarn companies that graciously donated yarn, thank you so much for all your support and quick response to all my requests.

I had wonderfully crafty crocheters help me make a lot of the samples for the book, and thus let me rest and not be a zombie. They are Rochelle Kaplan (my mom, I know she's the best!), Rebecca DeSensi, Virginia Boundy, Chie O'Briant, Wilma Keith, Rebecca Velasquez, Megan Granholm, Tiffany Roots, Michelle Grissam, and Cecily Keim.

Most important, I would like to thank my friends and family. All your thoughts and kind words have touched me very much these past few months. To Courtney, thank you for being my lifelong cheerleader, best friend, and sister. To my parents (all six of them), thank you for constantly supporting me. And to my family, Mark and Faye; you both mean more to me than I can ever express. Mark, I cannot tell you how blessed I am to have such an amazing partner for life. And yes, Faye, now we can go for a walk.

Dedication

To Faye, thank you for literally trotting into my life and changing it forever.

Table of Contents

Introduction

I have loved to crochet from the moment I picked up my first hook and ball of yarn. What I did not love right away was patterns. The jumble of abbreviations and words was just too much for my brain to process. It seemed that no matter how organized I was with crossing out rows I had finished or marking my place with post-it notes, I would still miss something and have to rip out. It got so frustrating that I decided to start designing my own projects, so I wouldn't miss a row or a stitch. The more I crocheted and designed the more I though there had to be a better way than the shorthand text that was being published.

It was about this time that I saw my first stitch dictionary with crochet symbols and at first glance I was hooked. I knew crochet diagrams and I were destined to go together, like peanut butter and jelly! For the first time, I could crochet a granny square and not get lost in the jumble of abbreviations. My immediate infatuation with diagrams comes from my daily life. I am a structural engineer, and every day I am working on drawings and details that show a picture of how the pieces of a building get put together. So when I finally saw symbol crochet and I could see what the stitch pattern looked like in a drawing, it was like I had found the blueprint into crochet that I had been searching for all that time. What I didn't realize then, was that a whole new world of crochet had just opened up to me. Now I could follow patterns from Japan, Portugal, and even Russia, not because I had learned three new languages, but because I could follow the crochet symbols without needing words.

My goal with this book is to open up this amazing new world of crochet to you as well and show you how easy and truly useful it is to use these diagrams. Along the way, I hope to entice you to crochet more and more of the patterns in the book by following the written words less and less, eventually relying solely on the crochet symbols. To help with this, I have gathered some of my favorite garments and accessories inspired by fashion magazines, by costumes in old '40s movies, and even by the quirky personalities in my family. In fact, you will notice along the way that I talk a lot about the women in my family because every pattern in this book is named after one of them. They are my support, my inspiration, and my source of creativity. So grab your hook and come join me on the sometimes kooky, but always fun adventure through *Blueprint Crochet*.

The Basics

If you are anything like me, you will blow by this section and move straight to the good stuff, the patterns! But STOP! Don't be like me. Sit down for a second. In this book, you are going to see things that many crochet patterns don't have: crochet symbols. Don't worry, by the end of this chapter you will be wondering what the big fuss was about and how you were ever able to live without them. Really, trust me, you will like learning this new trick.

○	# in circle indicates # of chains for loop
⬭	chain
•	slip stitch
+	single crochet
⊤	half double crochet
∓	double crochet
⧦	treble crochet
⧧	double treble
⋇	sc3tog
⬭	dc4tog
⬭	dc-cl
⋇	dc5tog
⊥	base stitch

Crochet Symbols

I am a visual person who works with graphics and drawings daily, so if you are anything like me you are going to love symbol crochet. The symbols have been around as long as crochet itself, although they may not always have looked exactly like what we use today. Symbols are a quick way to jot down the stitch pattern you are doing, and they allow you to see the big picture without photographs. They can also make a very complex pattern much easier to follow by simply showing you where to stitch.

A couple of years ago symbol crochet disappeared almost completely from American patterns. Thankfully, symbol crochet is becoming popular once again, thanks to computer programs that can easily generate the symbols, and global access to crochet design through the Internet. Designers, editors, and publishers are discovering the benefits of crochet symbols, including the international appeal of patterns that need no translation.

The key to understanding crochet symbols is that each symbol represents a crochet stitch. Yup, that's it. It's not rocket science; it's more like doing a paint-by-number. All you have to do is learn which symbol is which stitch. At first glance, these little symbols may seem arbitrary, but take another look and you may find it easier to relate the symbols to the stitches. Consider the chain stitch, a simple oval symbol. Think about making a chain stitch: it's a simple loop pulled through another loop. That loop looks a lot like an oval, right? Moving up the slip stitch is a filled-in dot; it is little and almost invisible, just like the stitch. The single crochet is a squat cross, again just like the stitch. Starting to see a trend? The half double crochet is slightly taller then the single crochet. The double crochet is taller then the half double, and it has an extra cross in its middle. From the double crochet up, the little cross tells you how many yarn overs you have before you insert your hook. Go ahead, make a double crochet. Now look at your stitch. Do you see the little cross in the middle of the stitch? Looks a lot like its symbol, huh? Each crochet symbol is actually a line-drawing replica of the shape and size of each stitch.

Understanding Granny Square Diagrams

Granny Square diagrams are like tiny maps. They show you what the motif will look like when it is completed, while giving you round by round directions to create it. To read the diagram, you need to start in the center, just like you would to crochet. Following the symbol key, crochet the stitches you see. The number circled in the center tells you how many chain stitches to crochet and join with a slip stitch to start. The other numbers on the diagram let you know where the beginning of each round is, so you can keep track of where you are. On my diagrams, I also like to color each round differently so that it's easy to see which round you are on.

Granny Squares Round by Round

Let's do an example together. Look at this granny square. You can see that it consists of 4 rounds and has an open, lacy construction. Now let's break it down round by round (for abbreviations list and illustrated instructions for stitches, see pgs 146-149).

Step One: Ch 6, sl st to first ch (circle made), do not turn. How do you know to chain 6? You can count the chain symbols (the ovals) or look at the circled number in the center.

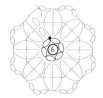

Step Two: Here you can clearly see which round you are on. The green stitches are the ones you are about to do, and the black ones are those you have already completed.

Ch 2, dc2tog in circle, [ch 3, dc-cl] in circle 7 times, ch 1, hdc into top of dc2tog, do not turn. Okay, stop. Does your granny look like the diagram?

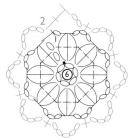

Step Three: [Ch 5, sc into top of ch-3 sp] 7 times, ch 2, dc into hdc on previous round, do not turn.

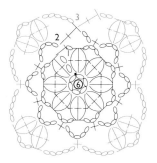

Step Four: *Ch 5, (dc-cl, ch 3, dc-cl) into next ch-5 sp, ch 5, sc in next ch-5 sp; rep from * twice more, ch 5, (dc-cl, ch 3, dc-cl) into next ch-5 sp, ch 2, dc into dc of previous round, do not turn.

Step Five: *Ch 5, sc into next ch-5 sp, ch 5, (sc, ch-5, sc) into ch-3 sp, ch 5, sc into next ch-5 sp; rep from * 3 more times, sl st to first ch-5 sp, fasten off, weave in ends. That's it, you got it! Now try it again without looking at the words.

Most of the patterns with granny squares have variations of the main granny square. These are either dividing the granny in half vertically, diagonally, or some combination of the two. They are crocheted in the same method as the one shown here, except at the end of a round you will turn your work.

Joining Granny Squares

The great thing about granny square projects is that you can start joining them at any place in the layout. You can start at the bottom edge and work your way up or start on the side and work to the other side or just work sporadically. Why is this? Flip to the Vogue Granny Motifs section (p. 52) and you'll notice that all the grannies are joined by crocheting as you go. Since you are building your garment one square at a time, it doesn't matter where you start.

You can join your grannies in one of two ways:
1. Crochet all the grannies you will need and leave a long tail at the end of each one. Now, unravel one side of the square to the corner of another and follow the Details section of the pattern to join them.
2. Crochet the granny square directly onto the previous one by following the joining details. The ultimate goal is to crochet an almost identical granny onto the previous one you were working on, by substituting the middle chain with a slip stitch.

Let's look at an example together. Crochet two of the Raeanne Granny Squares (p. 92). Now unravel the yarn to the corner ch-sp. As you can see, the corners are made from 5 chains. To connect these, ch 2, then sl st to the previous granny and then ch 2 more. This will make 5 stitches and provide the same corner as the previous granny and connect it. Now, continue crocheting the granny as before, until the next ch-sp. Slip stitch to the next ch-sp on the previous granny, ch 3, sc in the next ch-sp, ch 2, sl st to the next ch-sp on the previous granny, ch 2; rep from the sc. Ch 3, sl st to the next ch-sp on the previous granny, dc 3 times in the next ch-sp, ch 2, sl st to the next ch-sp on the previous granny, ch 2, sl st to tch, and fasten off. We have just connected the two grannies. As you can tell, it would have been just as easy to connect this granny while we were crocheting it

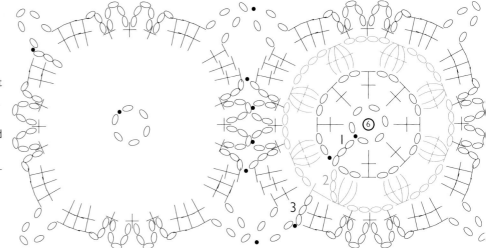

the first time rather then unraveling it. Now take a look at the grannies; the first one and the second one look exactly alike. The only difference is that the second one is joined to the first, but otherwise has the same amount of ch-sps and dcs.

I use crochet to join the granny squares together for two reasons. First, I hate sewing granny squares together, because it means that I'll have more ends to weave in. Second, when you crochet the grannies together, you never have to worry about the seam opening up. Crochet will always give you a strong seam, and with lacy grannies this is a definite benefit.

Understanding Stitch Pattern Diagrams

Just as the granny square diagrams are tiny drawings of how the motif will look when crocheted, the stitch pattern diagrams show you completed pattern repeats. To read the diagram, you need to start at the bottom foundation row just like you would to crochet. Begin by crocheting as many chains as the diagram shows. Do this by counting the number of chains before and after the stitch pattern repeat. Now, count how many chains are in the stitch pattern repeat and multiply it by how many stitch pattern repeats the pattern tells you to do. Add the two numbers together and you get your foundation chain count.

Following the symbol key, crochet the stitches you see for the first row. At the end of the row, turn and continue crocheting the stitches you see for the following rows. The numbers on the diagram let you know where the beginning of each row is so you can keep track of where you are. On my diagrams, I also like to color each row differently, so again, it's easy to see which row you are on. The stitch pattern repeat, or SR for short, is the combination of stitches that get repeated in every row. The row repeat, or RR for short, is the combination of rows that get repeated to create the crocheted fabric.

Let's do an example together. Look at the below stitch pattern diagram from the Courtney Corset Top (p. 138). You can see that it has two different rows. Now let's break it down row by row.

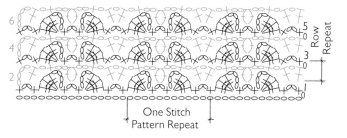

Step One: Ch 40, turn. How do you know to chain 40? You count the chain symbols (the ovals) before and after the stitch pattern repeat. Add this to the number of chains inside of the stitch pattern repeat, since the multiple is one.

Step Two: Sc in 2nd ch from hook, *ch 2, skip one ch, sc in next ch, skip 3 ch, (3 tr, ch 4, sc) in next ch; ch 2, skip one ch, (sc, ch 4, 3 tr) in next ch, skip 3 ch, sc in next ch; rep from * to last 2 ch, ch 2, skip one ch, sc in last ch, turn—18 tr. How many stitch pattern repeats (SR) are there? Yep, you are right, you can see them—3 SR.

Step Three: Ch 4 (counts as dc and ch 1), dc in ch 2-sp, *ch 1, skip 3 tr, sc in ch 4-sp, ch 2, dc2tog in ch 2-sp, ch 2, sc in ch 4-sp, ch 1, skip 3 tr, (dc, ch 1, dc) in ch2-sp; rep from * to end, turn. Now look at the crochet symbols for the row without looking at the written directions. Would you know where to put the stitches? Practice looking at the diagram until you do.

One Stitch
Pattern Repeat

Step Four: Ch 1, sc in dc, ch 2, skip ch, skip dc, *sc in ch1-sp, skip sc, (3 tr, ch 4, sc) in ch 2-sp, ch 2, skip dc2tog, (sc, ch 4, 3 tr) in ch 2-sp, skip sc, sc in ch 1-sp, ch 2, skip (dc, ch 1, dc); rep from * across, sc in last dc, turn—18 tr; 3 SR.

Now repeat the row repeat (RR) to the desired length. How do you know what the row repeat is for this pattern? Look at the diagram. It notes that Rows 2 and 3 make up the RR.

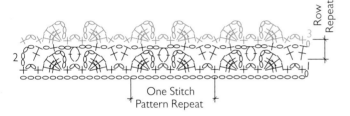

One Stitch
Pattern Repeat

Row Repeat

Stitch Pattern Plans into Diagrams

The last connection to understand is how you get from the plans to the stitch pattern detail diagrams. As you can see from the sleeve plan (above, right) from the Courtney Corset Top pattern, it shows how large the sleeve is and the overall amount of SRs and RRs it will take to create it. The plan will also direct you to the detail diagram that shows all the stitches in the sleeve. Now look at the sleeve stitch detail diagram, labeled "G," below. Notice how it looks upside down to the sleeve layout plan? That is because this sleeve is started at the shoulder and worked down

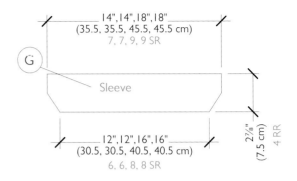

G

Sleeve

14", 14", 18", 18"
(35.5, 35.5, 45.5, 45.5 cm)
7, 7, 9, 9 SR

12", 12", 16", 16"
(30.5, 30.5, 40.5, 40.5 cm)
6, 6, 8, 8 SR

2⅞"
(7.5 cm)
4 RR

the arm. Also notice how the stitch diagram is colored. The stitches at the beginning and end of the rows are in color while the middle is black. This is because the middle is going to be the same as the main stitch diagram, and only the edges of the sleeve will diverge from the main stitch pattern. Just to make sure we are on the same page, how many SRs are there at the beginning of the large size of this sleeve? You can look at the sleeve plan, above, and see that the large has 9 SR as called out. Or you can look at the stitch diagram, labeled "G-Sleeves," below, and add 2 SR to the 7 SR called out to also get 9 SR. That's it. That's all there is to stitch pattern diagrams. Now that you have the basics down, you can practice your new skills with success as you venture into the patterns!

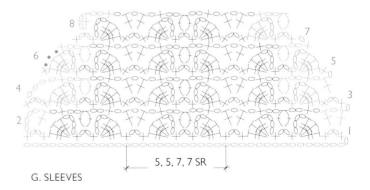

5, 5, 7, 7 SR

G. SLEEVES

How To Use This Book

Each pattern in this book is organized into sections, each with a specific function.

The Plans

Here you will find the final dimensions for the project as well as the number of granny squares or stitch pattern repeats that are in each section. You will also be alerted to any specifics you should be on the lookout for in the Construction section.

Foundation

This section will spell out the instructions for making the granny squares or stitch patterns that are the foundation upon which you build the project.

Construction

This section will go through the essentials for connecting the granny squares or shaping the stitch patterns into the project.

Finishing

This section includes information on how to make the final project look perfect.

As with all patterns, please read through it first before getting started. It is essential that you understand the steps you will need to complete, before jumping in. And with that, good luck; I hope that by the time you reach the end of this book you will be as delighted with crochet symbols as I am.

Effortless Motifs

Go take a look out your window. How many motifs do you see? Look closer, because they surround us, from the curving lines of a flower petal to the geometric grid of brick walls. Motifs are also everywhere in crochet, and in my opinion they are one of the coolest things about it. Within just a few rounds you can achieve a totally funky design that would have taken forever to do in knitting or embroidery. Since motifs are the essence of crochet, it is only fitting for me to help you get your feet wet in symbol crochet by working a few small motif projects. Each one is essentially made from one motif, but what makes it special is what you do with that one motif after you crochet it. By the end of this chapter, I am positive you will be well on your way to loving symbol crochet.

Heather Earrings & Necklace

Ever since I was a little girl, I have admired my big sister Heather's sense of style and the beautiful, intricate jewelry she wears. These motifs were born from that style I had always admired. Their delicate form is complemented by the modern sensibility of these oversize earrings and necklace. Perhaps when you wear them you will feel that same sense of awe that every little sister has for her amazing big sister.

Equipment

YARN: Crochet Thread (Size 10)

Shown: Aunt Lydia's Classic Crochet Thread
(100% Mercerized Cotton; 350 yd [320 m]/ 3 oz [85 g]): #12 black, 25 yd (23 m).

HOOKS: US7 (1.5 mm) steel and C/2 (2.75 mm) or hooks needed to obtain gauge.

NOTIONS (EARRINGS): 1 oz fabric stiffener; parchment paper; 2 sterling silver earring fish hooks; 12″ (30.5 cm) of 34 gauge wire.

NOTIONS (NECKLACE): 4 yd (3.6 m) of 6 1b. FireLine; 1 silver toggle clasp; 2 silver knot cups; 3 oz silver metallic size 10° seed beads; 3 oz opaque black size 6° seed beads; 1 oz fabric stiffener; parchment paper; paper towels; 1 lime green 20 mm glass disc; 2 lime green 10 x 12 mm glass barrel beads; 2 green 10 mm glass rondelles; 22 silver 3.5 mm spool-shaped spacer beads; sewing needle; round nose pliers; chain nose pliers.

SIZE: 1½ x 2″ (4 x 5 cm) = Earring Motif;
3¼ x 2¼″ (8.5 x 6 cm) = Necklace Motif.

> NOTES: *Use smaller hook for earrings and larger hook with 2 strands held together for necklace.*

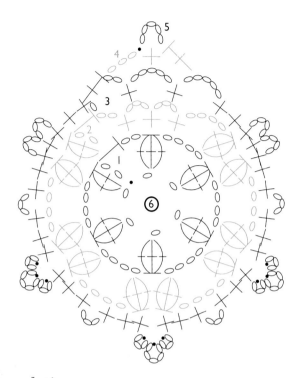

Foundation

Beginning Motif

See stitch diagram above for assistance.

Ch 6, sl st to first ch (ring made).

RND 1 (RS): Ch 2, dc2tog in ring, [ch 4, dc-cl in ring] 5 times, ch 2, hdc in beg dc2tog, do not turn.

RND 2: Ch 2, dc2tog around hdc, [(dc-cl, ch 4, dc-cl) in next ch-4 sp] 4 times, (dc-cl, ch 4, sc) in next ch-4 sp, ch 3, sc in next dc-cl, ch 3, sc in next ch-2 sp, ch 2, hdc in beg dc2tog, do not turn.

RND 3: Ch 1, 2 sc around hdc, (sc, ch 4, sc) in next dc-cl, ch 4, sc in next dc-cl, [(2 sc, ch 3, 2 sc) in next ch-4 sp, sc in next dc-cl, ch 3, sl st to first ch, ch 5, sl st to first ch, ch 3, sl st to first ch, sc in next dc-cl] 3 times, (2 sc, ch 3, 2 sc) in next ch-4 sp, sc in next dc-cl, ch 4, (sc, ch 4, sc) in next dc-cl, 2 sc in ch-4 sp, [ch 5, sc in next ch-3 sp] twice, ch 2, dc in first sc, turn.

ROW 4: Ch 3, sc in next ch-5 sp, dc in next ch-5 sp, turn.

ROW 5: Ch 5, sl st to ch-3 sp, fasten off, weave in ends.

Finishing

Dip finished pieces in fabric stiffener, pat excess stiffener off with paper towels, lay out to dry on parchment paper.

Earrings

(Make 2)

1. Using 6" (15.5 cm) of wire, string earring motif onto wire and wrap it around the top several times, then hold both ends of the wire together and string as many seed beads as desired (I used 1), to form a bail (see **Figure 1** for assistance).

2. Holding both ends of wire together, string one earring fish hook, pass both wires back through the seed bead(s)(**Figure 1**), and wrap both wires around the bail under the seed bead(s). Pinch closed with chain nose pliers.

Necklace

1. Cut 4 strands of FireLine, each 36" (91.5 cm) long (or desired finished length plus 6" [15.5 cm]). Holding all strands together, string necklace motif onto strands. Secure in place by holding the ends of all threads together and stringing the 20 mm disc to form a bail. You should have 8 strands extending from the bail (see **Figure 2** for assistance).

2. With 2 of the strands held together, string 15 spacer beads, 1 rondelle , 1 spacer bead, 1 rondelle, 2 spacer beads, 1 barrell bead, 74 size 6° seed beads, 1 spacer bead, and 1 size 10° seed bead (see **Figure 2** for assistance).

3. Pass the strands through the cup of the knot cup, and string 1 size 10° seed bead. Tie the strands into an overhand knot around the seed bead, and trim (**Figure 3**) (you may want to dab on some clear nail polish or cement to secure). Using chain nose pliers, gently push the cups of the knot cup closed around the knot (**Figure 4**).

4. String one side of the toggle clasp onto the hook of the knot cup, then grasp the hook with round nose pliers and curl it shut (**Figure 4**).

5. Holding the remaining 6 strands together, string one spacer bead, then separate strands and string desired amount of seed beads onto each individual strand (I used 70) (see **Figure 2** for assistance), leaving enough length at the end for the rest of the beads and the other half of the clasp.

6. Bring the 6 threads back together and string one spacer bead, 1 barrel, and enough size 6° seed beads to complete the necklace so that both sides are the same length (I used 74), 1 spacer bead, and 1 size 10° seed bead.

7. Repeat Step 3 to complete the other side of the clasp.

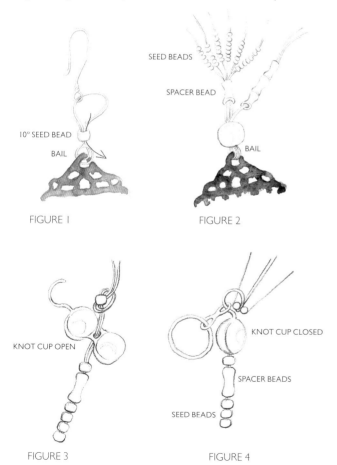

10° SEED BEAD

BAIL

FIGURE 1

SEED BEADS

SPACER BEAD

BAIL

FIGURE 2

KNOT CUP OPEN

FIGURE 3

KNOT CUP CLOSED

SPACER BEADS

SEED BEADS

FIGURE 4

Nicki Tote

My sister-in-law, Nicki, is the best friend you could ever want. She is the kind of person that will make something boring, like grocery shopping, the funniest experience you have had all year. Her beaming personality draws you toward her, and it was this feeling that was all the inspiration I needed to create this fantastic accessory. This tote is bold, sassy, and big enough to hold your life's necessities or your current crochet project.

Equipment

YARN: DK-weight (#3 Light)

Shown: SWTC Vickie Howell Collection, Rock (40% Soysilk, 30% Wool, 30% Hemp; 110 yd [100.5 m]/ 1.75 oz [50 g]): gwen (MC), 3 balls; billy (CC1), 1 ball; shirley (CC2), 1 ball.

HOOK: G/6 (4.25 mm) or hook needed to obtain gauge.

NOTIONS: Tapestry needle; 3 silver hoops about 2″ (5 cm) in diameter; 2 yd (1.8 m) of fabric for lining; matching sewing thread; invisible thread; sewing needle; optional: sewing machine.

GAUGE: 1 7/8″ (5 cm) = Circle Motif Diameter.

SIZE: Finished size is 15 x 10″ (38 x 25.5 cm), excluding strap.

> NOTES: *Instructions for sewing the lining are given for hand sewing.*
> *You can also use a sewing machine and a standard machine stitch.*

The Plans

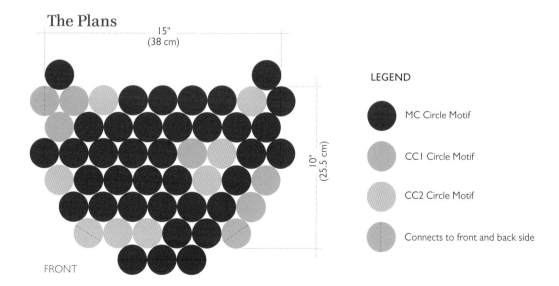

15"
(38 cm)

10"
(25.5 cm)

FRONT

LEGEND

● MC Circle Motif

● CC1 Circle Motif

● CC2 Circle Motif

● Connects to front and back side

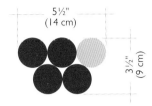

5½"
(14 cm)

3½"
(9 cm)

FLAP

15"
(38 cm)

Attach Flap

11¼"
(29 cm)

BACK

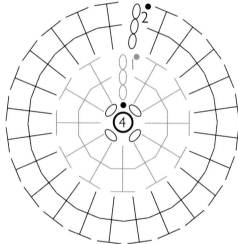

CIRCLE MOTIF

Foundation

Circle Motif

Make 73 MC, 12 CC1, 15 CC2.

Follow stitch diagram to make motif. Leave a long tail for seaming.

Straps

With MC, ch 8.

ROW 1: Sc in 2nd ch from hook, sc in each ch across, turn—7 sc.

ROW 2: Ch 1, sc in each sc across, turn.

Repeat Row 2 until the strap measures 21" (53.5 cm). Join CC1, repeat Row 2 for 10" (25.5 cm). Join CC2, repeat Row 2 for 4" (10 cm), fasten off, leaving a long tail for seaming.

Finishing

Using long tail ends and tapestry needle, sew motifs together as shown in the layouts above. Once sewn together, pin layouts down, spritz with water, and allow to dry. Fold lining fabric in half along the grain and trace front and back layout pieces onto fabric, adding an additional 1" (2.5 cm) to top edge of each piece for hem. Cut out pieces through both layers of fabric to make two lining bags (be sure to match up one front with one back).

Working with one set at a time, pin right sides of front and back together. Using matching thread, backstitch each set together using ⅜" (1 cm) seam allowance, leave top open. Turn one of the bags right side out and press with iron to flatten seams. On each lining piece press top edges down ½" (1.3 cm), then fold over another ½" (1.3 cm) and press. Place one lining bag inside the other with wrong sides together, so that folded edges match up. Backstitch along top edge, then move down ¼" (6 mm) and backstitch around again.

Using extra yarn and tapestry needle, sew crocheted layouts together in the following order: front to back and flap to back. Weave in loose ends. Using invisible thread and sewing needle, sew bag to lining along top edge.

Using extra yarn and tapestry needle, sew one silver hoop to each side of bag by wrapping yarn around hoop and securing to one crocheted circle on each side (see image at right). Sew remaining ring to bottom of front flap. Weave tail ends of yarn back into crocheted motifs and trim. Thread strap through both rings. Using long tail end and tapestry needle, whipstitch ends of strap together.

Julie Cuff

Do some patterns just grab you and pull you toward them? How about colors? And jewelry? Well, for me, all three were flashing in my mind, but I couldn't quite decide how I wanted to combine them. I knew I wanted a snazzy cuff with a spiraling flower motif in bold colors. Then one afternoon I was e-mailing my sister-in-law, Julie, and an advertisement for a new fabric print popped up on my screen. There it was! The inspiration I needed to combine my ideas into the exact cuff I wanted. This cuff can be worn stiff with a pretty little silver clasp or soft with sweet buttons. Why not try both on for size?

Equipment

YARN: Crochet Thread (Size 3)

Shown: Aunt Lydia's Fashion Crochet Thread

(100% Mercerized Cotton; 150 yd [137.5 m]/ 3 oz. [85 g]): scarlet, 50 yds (46 m).

HOOK: D/3 (3.25 mm) or hook needed to obtain gauge.

NOTIONS: Tapestry needle; option 1: two ¼" (1 cm) round pearl buttons;

option 2: 1 oz (28.5 g) fabric stiffener; parchment paper; paper towels;

soda can (or any wrist mold); ½ x ¾" (1.5 x 2 cm) jewelry clasp.

SIZE: 6½ x 2" (16.5 x 5 cm) = Cuff.

NOTES: *The center flower motif is worked in the round, so you do not need to turn at the end of each round. The sides are worked in rows.*

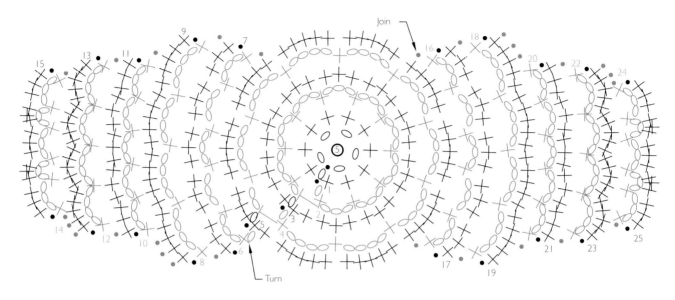

Construction

Julie Motif

Follow stitch diagram above for cuff.

Finishing

Join yarn to edge with right side facing, sl st around edge of cuff evenly, fasten off, weave in ends.

Option 1: Join yarn to beginning of Row 25 with sl st, sl st in next 3 sts, ch 5, skip 1 st, sl st in next 5 sts, ch 5, skip 1 st, sl st to end, fasten off, weave in ends. Sew buttons to opposite end of cuff using ch-5 loops as a guide.

Option 2: Dip finished pieces in fabric stiffener, pat excess stiffener off with paper towels. Wrap motif around soda can. Wait until the cuff is semi-dry, remove can (about an hour). Bend ends flat, set on parchment paper to dry. Sew one end of jewelry clasp to each end of cuff.

✳ Quick Stitch Patterns

One of the things that drew me to crochet was how quickly I could whip up great projects. Other crafts seemed to take me twice as long to do similar projects. In the beginning, when I wanted to try every new technique I came across, I loved that in one night I could have a scarf or a hat or a toy. For this reason, I wanted to share my love of quick stitch patterns. There are those of you who are like me and need some quick projects to further develop your symbol crochet reading skills. All the projects in this chapter were developed to take you deeper and deeper into loving crochet diagrams, yet they will not take you very long to complete. So go ahead and jump in, and you'll soon find yourself with a great scarf, wrap, tunic, or belt.

Madison Scarf

Do you have a person in your life that is always happy and bright? Well, I do. See, my 2-year-old niece, Madison, is one of those kids that can turn any grumpy Gus into a smiley Sam just with her giggle. She loves putting on a show for you, or talking on the phone, and just brightening your day. That's why I designed this scarf with its fun shapes and beautiful bright color. Hopefully, it will be a happy influence, so that whenever you wear it, it will put a smile on your face.

Equipment

YARN: Worsted-weight (#4 Medium)

Shown: Blue Sky Cotton by Blue Sky Alpacas, Dyed Cotton (100% Cotton; 150 yd [137 m]/ 3.5 oz [100 g]): #630 caribbean, I hank.

HOOK: K/10½ (6.5 mm) or hook needed to obtain gauge.

NOTIONS: Tapestry needle.

GAUGE: 4½″ (11.5 cm) = Beginning Motif.

FINISHED SIZE: 4½ x 65¼″ (11.5 x 166 cm)

NOTES: *Start with beginning motif and then continue to motifs A thru C to desired length, ending with motif B. Complete motif D, then start filling in opposite side of motifs to beginning.*

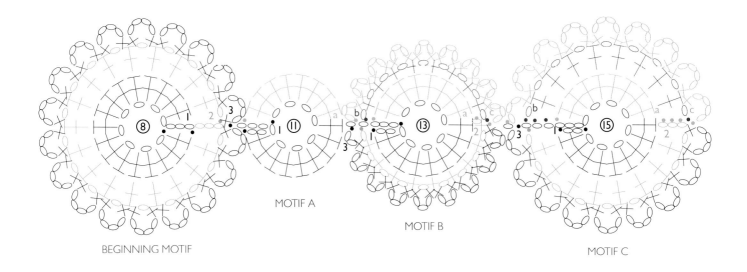

BEGINNING MOTIF

MOTIF A

MOTIF B

MOTIF C

Construction

See stitch diagram above for assistance.

Beginning Motif

Ch 8, sl st to first ch (ring made).

RND 1 (RS): Ch 3 (count as one dc), dc in ring 17 times total, turn—18 dc.

RND 2: Ch 4 (counts as one dc and ch 1), (dc, ch 1) in next dc and in each dc around, sl st to first dc, turn—18 dc.

RND 3: Ch 1, (sc, ch 4, sc) in each ch-1 sp around, sl st to first sc, do not fasten off, cont to Motif A.

Motif A

Ch 11, sl st to 8th ch from hook (ring made).

RND 1: Ch 2, sl st to first ch of beg ch-11, dc in ring 9 times total, do not fasten off, cont to Motif B.

Motif B

Ch 13, sl st to 8th ch from hook (ring made).

RND 1: Ch 2, skip 2 ch of beg ch-13, sl st to next ch, dc in ring 9 times total, turn.

RND 2: Ch 1, sc in first dc, ch 1, [sc in next dc, ch 1] 8 times, sl st to 2nd ch of beg ch-13, turn—9 sc.

RND 3: Sl st to first ch of beg ch-13, ch 2, sc in next ch-1 sp, (sc, ch 3, sc) in each ch-1 sp around, do not fasten off, cont to Motif C.

Motif C

Ch 15, sl st to 8th ch from hook (ring made).

RND 1: Ch 2, skip 2 ch of beg ch-15, sl st to next ch, dc in ring 9 times, turn.

RND 2: Ch 4 (counts as dc and ch-1 sp), (dc, ch 1) in next dc and in each dc around, skip 2 ch of beg ch-15, sl st to next ch, turn—9 dc.

RND 3: Sl st to first ch of beg ch-15, ch 3, sc in next ch-1 sp, (sc, ch 4, sc) in each ch-1 sp around, do not fasten off, cont to Motif A.

Rep Motifs A–C 4 more times, rep Motif A and B once more, cont to Motif D.

Motif D

Ch 15, sl st to 8th ch from hook (ring made).

RND 1: Ch 2, skip 2 ch of beg ch-15, sl st to next ch, dc in ring 17 times, sl st in 5th ch of beg ch-15, turn—17 dc.

RND 2: Sl st in next 3 ch, ch 1, (dc, ch 1) in next dc and in each dc around, skip 2 ch of beg ch-15, sl st to next ch, turn—17 dc.

RND 3: Sl st to first ch of beg ch-15, ch 3, sc in next ch-1 sp, (sc, ch 4, sc) in each ch-1 sp around to last ch-1 sp, sc in ch-1 sp, ch 3, sl st to first ch of beg ch-15, do not fasten off, cont to Motif B opposite side.

Motif B Opposite Side

RND A: Sl st in last sc of rnd 3, sl st in first sc of Rnd 2, dc in ring 8 times total, skip 2 ch of beg ch-13, sl st to next ch.

RND B: Sl st to next ch, ch 1, (sc, ch 1) in next dc and in each dc around, sl st to last sc of Rnd 2, turn.

RND C: Ch 3, sc in ch-1 sp, (sc, ch 3, sc) in each ch-1 sp around to last ch-1 sp, sc in last ch-1 sp, ch 3, sl st to first ch of beg ch-13, do not fasten off, cont to Motif A opposite side.

Motif A Opposite Side

RND A: Dc in ring 8 times total, skip 2 ch of beg ch-11, sl st in next ch, do not fasten off, cont to Motif C opposite side.

Motif C Opposite Side

RND A: Sl st in last sc of Rnd 3, [sl st in tch of Rnd 2] 3 times, dc in ring 8 times, skip 2 ch of beg ch-15, sl st in next ch.

RND B: Sl st in next 3 ch, ch 1, (dc, ch 1) in next dc and in each dc around, skip 2 ch of Rnd 2 tch, sl st to next ch, turn.

RND C: Ch 4, sc in ch-1 sp, (sc, ch 4, sc) in each ch-1 sp around to last ch-1 sp, sc in last ch-1 sp, ch 3, sl st to first ch of beg ch-15, do not fasten off, cont to Motif B opposite side.

Rep motifs to beginning, end with Motif A. Fasten off, weave in ends.

Isabella Wrap

My 5-year-old niece, Isabella, loves picking out just the right style for every activity, even sleeping. She would have been right at home during my grandmother's era, when every woman was expected to be just like Isabella. Although I am not half as together as she is, I still admire those well-dressed ladies right down to their bedclothes. This wrap takes its inspiration from the 1940s bed jackets that wrapped in the front to accentuate your curves, making you look put together even though you just woke up. The addition of the geometric trim gives this piece a contemporary edge that updates the silhouette.

Equipment

YARN: Sport-weight (#2 Fine)

Shown: Blue Sky Alpaca Sport Weight (100% Baby Alpaca; 110 yd [100.5 m]/1.75 oz [50 g]):
#524 nickel (MC), 9 hanks; #500 natural (CC), 2 hanks.

HOOKS: L/11 (8 mm) and G/6 (4.25 mm) hooks or hooks needed to obtain gauge.

NOTIONS: Tapestry needle; stitch markers.

GAUGE: 11 st by 8 rows = 4 x 4″ (10 x 10 cm) in hdc with larger hook.

The Plans

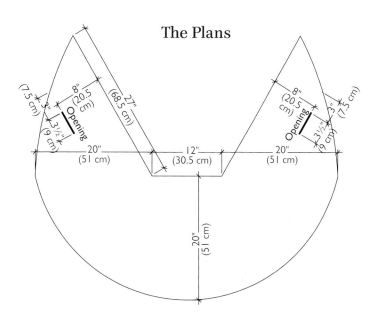

Construction

Body

With larger hook and MC, ch 173. Turn.

ROW 1 (RS): Hdc in 2nd ch from hook, hdc in the next 68 ch, 3 hdc in next ch (pm in first and third st), hdc in the next 30 ch, 3 hdc in next ch (pm in first and third st), hdc in each ch to end, turn—176 hdc.

ROW 2: Ch 1, sc in first hdc, hdc in each hdc across to last hdc, sc in last hdc, turn—174 hdc.

ROW 3: Sl st in sc, sl st in next hdc, sc in next hdc, hdc in next 68 hdc, 3 hdc in next hdc (pm in center st), hdc in next 32 hdc, 3 hdc in next hdc (pm in center st), hdc in each hdc to last 2 hdc, sc in next hdc, leave remaining st unworked, turn—174 hdc.

ROW 4: Sl st in sc, sl st in next hdc, sc in next hdc, hdc in next 74 hdc, [2 hdc in next hdc, hdc in next 4 hdc] 5 times, hdc in each hdc to last 2 hdc, sc in next hdc, leave rem st unworked, turn—175 hdc.

ROW 5: Sl st in sc, sl st in next hdc, sc in next hdc, hdc in each hdc to 1st marker from 4 rows below, 3 hdc in next hdc (pm in first st), hdc in each hdc to 2nd marker, 3 hdc in next hdc (pm in last st), hdc in each hdc to 3rd marker, 3 hdc in next hdc (pm in first st), hdc in each hdc to 4th marker, 3 hdc in next hdc (pm in last st), hdc in each hdc across to last 2 hdc, sc in next hdc, leave rem sts unworked, turn—179 hdc.

ROW 6: Ch 1, sc in hdc, hdc in each hdc across to last hdc, sc in next hdc, turn—177 hdc.

ROW 7: Sl st in sc, sl st in next hdc, sc in next hdc, hdc in each hdc to 1st marker from 4 rows below, 3 hdc in next hdc (pm in center st), hdc in each hdc to 2nd marker, 3 hdc in next hdc (pm in center st), hdc in each hdc across to last 2 hdc, sc in next hdc, leave last sts unworked, turn—177 hdc.

ROW 8: Sl st in sc, sl st in next hdc, sc in next hdc, hdc in next 74 hdc, [2 hdc in next hdc, hdc in next 5 hdc] 5 times, hdc in each hdc to last 2 hdc, sc in next hdc, leave rem st unworked, turn—178 hdc.

ROWS 9–11: Rep Rows 5–7—180 hdc.

ROW 12: Sl st in sc, sl st in next hdc, sc in next hdc, hdc in next 74 hdc, [2 hdc in next hdc, hdc in next 6 hdc] 5 times, hdc in each hdc to last 2 hdc, sc in next hdc, leave rem st unworked, turn—181 hdc.

ROWS 13–15: Rep Rows 5–7—183 hdc.

ROW 16: Sl st in sc, sl st in next hdc, sc in next hdc, hdc in next 73 hdc, [2 hdc in next hdc, hdc in next 7 hdc] 5 times, hdc in each hdc to last 2 hdc, sc in next hdc, leave rem st unworked, turn—184 hdc.

ROWS 17–19: Rep Rows 5–7—186 hdc.

ROW 20: Sl st in sc, sl st in next hdc, sc in next hdc, hdc in next 7 hdc, ch 9, skip 9 hdc, hdc in next 57 hdc, [2 hdc in next hdc, hdc in next 8 hdc] 5 times, hdc in each hdc to last 18 hdc, ch 9, skip 9 hdc, hdc in next 7 hdc, sc in next hdc, leave rem st unworked, turn—169 hdc.

ROW 21: Sl st in sc, sl st in next hdc, sc in next hdc, hdc in each hdc to ch-9 sp, 9 hdc in ch-9 sp, hdc in each hdc to 1st marker from 3 rows below, 3 hdc in next hdc (pm in first st), hdc in each hdc to 2nd marker, 3 hdc in next hdc (pm in last st), hdc in each hdc to 3rd marker, 3 hdc in next hdc (pm in first st), hdc in each hdc to 4th marker, 3 hdc in next hdc (pm in last st), hdc to ch-9 sp, 9 hdc in ch-9 sp, hdc in each hdc across to last 2 hdc, sc in next hdc, leave last sts unworked, turn—191 hdc.

ROWS 22–23: Rep Rows 6–7—189 hdc.

ROW 24: Sl st in sc, sl st in next hdc, sc in next hdc, hdc in next 72 hdc, [2 hdc in next hdc, hdc in next 9 hdc] 5 times, hdc in each hdc to last 2 hdc, sc in next hdc, leave rem st unworked, turn—190 hdc.

ROWS 25–27: Rep Rows 5–7—192 hdc.

Border

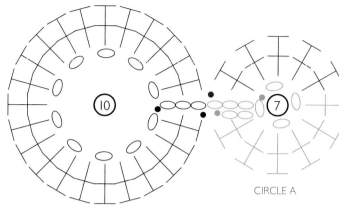

BEGINNING CIRCLE

CIRCLE A

ROW 28: Sl st in sc, sl st in next hdc, sc in next hdc, hdc in next 71 hdc, [2 hdc in next hdc, hdc in next 10 hdc] 5 times, hdc in each hdc to last 2 hdc, sc in next hdc, leave rem st unworked, turn—193 hdc.

ROWS 29–31: Rep Rows 5–7—195 hdc.

ROW 32: Sl st in sc, sl st in next hdc, sc in next hdc, hdc in next 71 hdc, [2 hdc in next hdc, hdc in next 11 hdc] 5 times, hdc in each hdc to last 2 hdc, sc in next hdc, leave rem st unworked, turn—196 hdc.

ROWS 33–35: Rep Rows 5–7—198 hdc.

ROW 36: Sl st in sc, sl st in next hdc, sc in next hdc, hdc in next 71 hdc, [2 hdc in next hdc, hdc in next 12 hdc] 5 times, hdc in each hdc to last 2 hdc, sc in next hdc, leave rem st unworked, turn—199 hdc.

ROWS 37–39: Rep Rows 5–7—201 hdc.

ROW 40: Sl st in sc, sl st in next hdc, sc in next hdc, hdc in next 70 hdc, [2 hdc in next hdc, hdc in next 13 hdc] 5 times, hdc in each hdc to last 2 hdc, sc in next hdc, leave rem st unworked, fasten off, weave in ends—202 hdc.

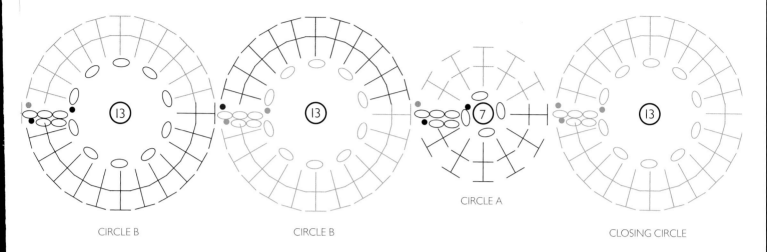

CIRCLE B   CIRCLE B   CIRCLE A   CLOSING CIRCLE

Edging

Change to smaller hook, with RS facing, join yarn in any st, ch 1, sc evenly around wrap, fasten off, weave in ends.

ROW 1: With WS facing, join yarn at top edge, ch 1, sc evenly across top, turn.

ROW 2: Ch 1, sc evenly across top edge, fasten off, weave in ends.

Border

See stitch diagram above for assistance.

With smaller hook and CC:

BEGINNING CIRCLE: Ch 10, sl st to first ch to form ring, ch 3, 23 dc in ring, sl st to top of ch 3, do not turn, cont to Circle A.

CIRCLE A: Ch 7, sl st to 4th ch to form ring, ch 2, sl st to first ch, 6 dc in ring, do not turn, cont to Circle B.

CIRCLE B: Ch 13, sl st to 10th ch to form ring, ch 2, sl st to first ch, 12 dc in ring, do not turn, cont to next circle.

Rep Circle B, rep [Circle A, Circle B, Circle B] 34 times, rep Circle A again.

CLOSING CIRCLE: Ch 13, sl st to 10th ch to form ring, ch 2, sl st to first ch, 23 dc in ring, sl st to last ch of beg ch-13, cont to Half Circle A.

HALF CIRCLE A: 5 dc in ring, sl st to 1st ch of beg ch-7, cont to Half Circle B.

HALF CIRCLE B: 11 dc in ring, sl st to 1st ch of beg ch-13, cont to next circle.

Work Half Circles A and B in their respective circles to end. Fasten off, weave in ends.

Finishing

Block body to dimensions in plan (see p. 37). With RS facing, pin border to bottom edge, leaving 9 circles unattached at each end to become the ties. With CC and tapestry needle, whipstitch to edge of body.

Maureen Tunic

My family is spread out all over the world; in fact, my brother's family is living in Bangladesh right now. Since we travel to such interesting locales to visit family, I wanted to create a top for my globe-trekking sister-in-law, Maureen, so that she would feel at home whether she was in Dhaka, Brussels, or San Francisco. The easy stitch repeat and simple construction make this a great project to crochet, whether you are traveling to exotic locales or simply enjoying an afternoon at home.

Equipment

YARN: **Sport-weight (#2 Fine)**

Shown: Louet Euroflax Sportweight (100% Wet Spun Linen; 270 yd [247 m]/ 3.5 oz [100 g]): french blue (MC), 5 (7, 8, 10) hanks; cream (CC1), 1 (1, 1, 1) hanks; aqua (CC2), 1 (1, 2, 2) hanks.

HOOK: G/6 (4.25 mm) or hook needed to obtain gauge.

NOTIONS: Tapestry needle; stitch markers; pins.

GAUGE: 22 sts (11 SR) and 14 rows (7 RR) = 4 x 4″ (10.5 x 10.5 cm) in V Stack Stitch Pattern.

SIZE: Small (Medium, Large, X-Large) fits 34 (38, 42, 46)″, (86.5 [96.5, 107, 117] cm) bust circumference.

Tunic shown in small.

> NOTES: *Garment is constructed in one piece by starting at the front and working up the right side of the body to the back of the neck, then continuing up left side to back of neck and joining sides to finish working down back. Edging is added in the last step.*

The Plans

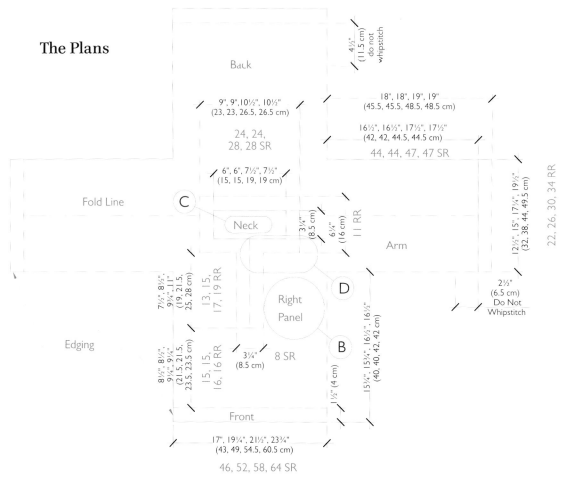

Back

4½"
(11.5 cm)
do not
whipstitch

9", 9", 10½", 10½"
(23, 23, 26.5, 26.5 cm)

24, 24,
28, 28 SR

18", 18", 19", 19"
(45.5, 45.5, 48.5, 48.5 cm)

16½", 16½", 17½", 17½"
(42, 42, 44.5, 44.5 cm)

44, 44, 47, 47 SR

6", 6", 7½", 7½"
(15, 15, 19 cm)

Fold Line

C

Neck

3¾"
(8.5 cm)

6¼" (16 cm)

11 RR

Arm

12½", 15", 17¼", 19½"
(32, 38, 44, 49.5 cm)

22, 26, 30, 34 RR

7½", 8½", 11"
9¾", 11"
(19, 21.5, 25, 28 cm)

13, 15,
17, 19 RR

D

Right
Panel

2½"
(6.5 cm)
Do Not
Whipstitch

Edging

8½", 8½",
9¼", 9¼"
(21.5, 21.5,
23.5, 23.5 cm)

15, 15,
16, 16 RR

3¼"
(8.5 cm)

8 SR

15¾", 15¾", 16½", 16½"
(40, 40, 42, 42 cm)

B

1½" (4 cm)

Front

17", 19¼", 21½", 23¾"
(43, 49, 54.5, 60.5 cm)

46, 52, 58, 64 SR

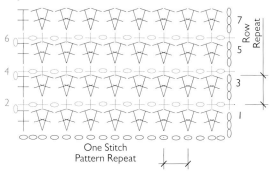

7
6
5
4
3
2
1

Row Repeat

One Stitch
Pattern Repeat

A. V STACK PATTERN

Foundation

V Stack Stitch Pattern

See stitch diagram A for assistance. Ch 27.

ROW 1: 2 dc in 5th ch from hook (4 skipped ch count as one dc and one ch), *skip next ch, 2 dc in next ch; rep from * across to last 2 ch, skip next ch, dc in last ch, turn—24 dc, 11 SR.

ROW 2: Ch 1, sc in first dc, *ch 1, sc in between 2-dc group; rep from * across, ch 1, sc in last dc, turn.

ROW 3: Ch 3, skip sc and ch-1 sp, *2 dc in next sc, skip ch-1 sp; rep from * across, dc in last sc, turn.

Rep Rows 2–3 to desired length.

B. RIGHT PANEL

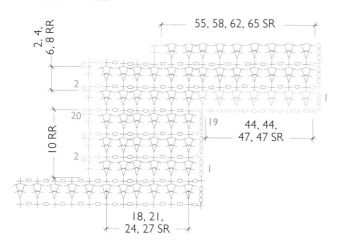

2, 4, 6, 8 RR

55, 58, 62, 65 SR

2

20

10 RR

19

44, 44, 47, 47 SR

2

18, 21, 24, 27 SR

Construction

Front

With MC, ch 97 (109, 121, 133); turn.

ROW 1 (RS): Follow Row 1 of V Stack stitch pattern—94 (106, 118, 130) dc, 46 (52, 58, 64) SR.

Rep Rows 2–3 of V Stack stitch pattern 14 (14, 15, 15) times.

Rep Row 2 once more before continuing.

Right Panel Neck Opening

See stitch diagram B for help on shaping front.

ROW 1: Follow Row 3 of V Stack stitch pattern for 18, (21, 24, 27) sc, skip next ch-1 sp, dc in next sc, turn, leave remaining sts unworked for opposite panel—18 (21, 24, 27) SR.

Rep Rows 2–3 of V Stack stitch pattern 9 times.

NEXT ROW: Rep Row 2 to end, ch 92 (92, 98, 98) for arm, turn.

Right Arm

ROW 1: Follow Row 1 of V Stack stitch pattern over ch sts, 2 dc in first sc, cont in Row 3 of V Stack stitch pattern to end—63 (66, 72, 75) SR.

Rep Rows 2–3 of V Stack stitch pattern 2 (4, 6, 8) times.

Rep Row 2 once more before continuing.

C. NECK OPENING

← 24, 24, 28, 28 SR →

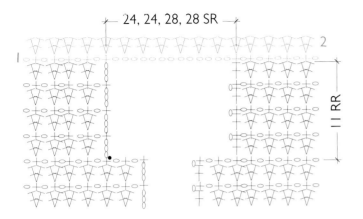

NEXT ROW: Follow Row 3 of V Stack stitch pattern for 55, (58, 62, 65) sc, skip next ch-1 sp, dc in next sc, turn, leave remaining sts unworked for neck opening—55 (58, 62, 65) SR.

Rep Rows 2–3 of V Stack stitch pattern 10 times, fasten off, weave in ends.

Left Panel Neck Opening

ROW 1: With RS facing, join new yarn with sl st to left side panel, 9 sc from right side, ch 3, cont in Row 3 of V Stack stitch pattern to end—18 (21, 24, 27) SR.

Rep Rows 2–3 of V Stack stitch pattern 9 times.

Rep Row 2 once more.

Left Arm

ROW 1 (RS): Lay down working yarn, join new yarn with sl st to first st at the left side edge (beginning of previous row), ch 90 (90, 96, 96), fasten off. Pick up working yarn again, cont in Row 3 of V Stack stitch to last sc, 2 dc in last sc, skip first ch, 2 dc in next ch, cont in Row 1 of V Stack stitch pattern over remaining ch to end—63 (66, 72, 75) SR.

Rep Rows 2–3 of V Stack stitch pattern 2 (4, 6, 8) times.

Rep Row 2 once more before continuing, fasten off, weave in ends.

NEXT ROW (RS): Skip 8 (8, 10, 10) sc, join yarn in next sc with sl st, ch 3 (counts as one dc), cont in Row 3 of V Stack stitch pattern to end—55 (58, 62, 65) SR.

Rep Rows 2–3 of V Stack stitch pattern 10 times.

Neck Joining and Arms

See stitch diagram C for help on neck joining.

ROW 1 (WS): Cont in Row 2 of V Stack stitch pattern to last dc on left side, ch 49, (49, 57, 57) sc in first dc of right side, cont in Row 2 of V Stack stitch pattern to end.

ROW 2: Follow Row 3 of V Stack stitch pattern to large ch-sp, 2 dc in last sc before ch-sp, skip first ch, 2 dc in next ch, cont in Row 1 of V Stack stitch pattern across to last ch, skip last ch 2, dc in next sc, cont in Row 3 of V Stack stitch pattern to end—136 (142, 154, 160) SR.

Rep Rows 2–3 of V Stack stitch pattern 7 (9, 11, 13) times, fasten off, weave in ends.

Back

ROW 1: Skip 44 (44, 47, 47) SR, join yarn with sl st to next dc, ch 1, sc in next dc, [ch 1, sc in between 2 dc group] 46 (52, 58, 64) times, ch 1, sc in next dc, turn, leave remaining sts unworked.

ROW 2: Rep Row 3 of V Stack stitch pattern.

Rep Rows 2–3 of V Stack stitch pattern 24 (24, 25, 25) times, fasten off, weave in ends.

Finishing

With RS facing, whipstitch arm and side seams closed with tapestry needle. Leave 2½" (6.5 cm) at end of arm open and 4½" (11.5 cm) at bottom of body open. Turn right side out.

Collar

See diagram D for assistance on corners.

With RS facing, join CC1 yarn with sl st at center back of neck opening.

RND 1: Ch 1, sc evenly around opening, sl st to first sc, turn.

RND 2: Ch 1, sc in each sc, sc3tog in inside corners, 3 sc in outside corners, sl st to first sc, turn, fasten off, weave in ends.

RND 3: Join CC2 with sl st at center back of neck opening, ch 3 (counts as one dc), dc in each sc, dc5tog in inside corners, 5 dc in outside corners, sl st to first dc, turn.

RND 4: Ch 3 (counts as one dc), dc in each dc, dc5tog in inside corners, 3 dc in outside corners, sl st to first dc, turn.

Rep Rnd 4 once more, fasten off, weave in ends.

Collar and Body Edging

With RS facing, join CC1 yarn with sl st in any st.

RND 1: Ch 1, sc evenly around. Opening, sl st to first sc, turn.

RND 2: Ch 1, sc in each sc around. At split: work 3 sc in outside corner st, sc in each st to center point of split, sc3tog (pm) over center 3 sc, sl st to first sc, turn, fasten off and weave in ends.

RND 3: Join CC2 with sl st, ch 3 (counts as dc), dc in each st of straight sections. At split: 3 dc in center st of outside corner group, dc in each st to 6 sts before marked st, hdc in next 3 sts, sc in next 2 sts, sc3tog (pm) over next 3 sts, sc in next 2 sts, hdc in next 3 sts, dc in each st to next corner group, 3 dc in center st of next corner group, sl st to first dc, turn.

Rep Rnd 3 twice more, fasten off, weave in ends.

Machine wash and dry to desired softness. Remove from dryer when still damp, pin to schematic size, and allow to dry.

D. EDGING

Nora Belt

I love fashion magazines. It's so much fun trying to spot trends in colors, styles, and fabrics before the experts do. Sometimes, though, the magazines get me into trouble, like when I see something that I just have to have, even though my pocketbook may not agree. Luckily, I don't have to worry too much, because I know crochet will come to my rescue. This belt was inspired by a belt I saw in one of my favorite magazines and created in crochet for my niece Nora, and for you.

Equipment

YARN: Crochet Thread (Size 3)

Shown: Aunt Lydia's Cable Crochet Thread (100% Mercerized Cotton;
200 yd [183 m]/3 oz [85 g]): black, 1 ball.

HOOK: E/4 (3.5 mm) or hook needed to obtain gauge.

NOTIONS: Tapestry needle; stitch markers; 1 oz (28.5 g) fabric stiffener;
blocking pins; 1½ x 1½″ (4 x 4 cm) belt buckle.

GAUGE: 2 ¼ x 1 ¾″ (6 x 4.5 cm) = Beginning Motif.

SIZE: Small (Medium, Large, X-Large) measures 27 (29 ¼, 31 ½, 33 ¾)″
(68.5 [74.5, 80, 86] cm) (after blocking but pre-stretch).
Final measurement after stretching and including buckle is
32½ (35, 37½, 40)″ [82.5 (89, 95.5, 102) cm] long.
Belt shown in size Small.

> NOTES: *Mark corner ch sts with stitch markers as you crochet; it will make finding the corners much easier. This belt tends to stretch over time. To account for this, block each motif slightly smaller than the actual desired measurement so that your final length is correct.*

The Plans

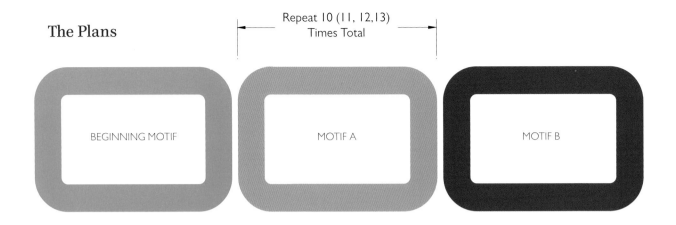

Repeat 10 (11, 12,13)
Times Total

BEGINNING MOTIF

MOTIF A

MOTIF B

Construction

Following stitch diagrams above right, make Beg Motif, work
bottom half of Motif A 10 (11, 12, 13) times, make Motif B, work
top half of Motif A across.

Finishing

Links

Make 11 (12, 13, 14).

Ch 15.

ROW 1 (RS): Hdc in 3rd ch from hook, hdc in each remaining ch to
     end. Fasten off, leave long tail for weaving in ends—13 hdc.

Pin belt down with blocking pins. Block each motif to 2¼ x 1¾"
(5.5 x 4.5 cm). Mix 1 part water with 1 part fabric stiffener in
spray bottle. Spritz belt with stiffening solution. Allow to dry.
For a stiffer belt, re-spray with stiffening solution. Wrap a link
around first two motifs, whipstitch ends together, and weave in
ends. Repeat for every motif. Whipstitch one belt buckle end
to beginning and last motif.

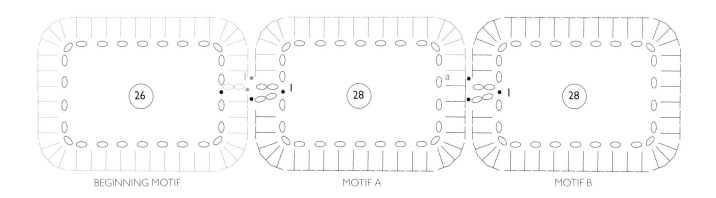

BEGINNING MOTIF   MOTIF A   MOTIF B

Vogue Granny Motifs

Say it with me now: granny squares are not just for afghans. LOUDER! GRANNY SQUARES ARE NOT JUST FOR AFGHANS! They can be crocheted in any fiber and made into any garment. My goal is to convince you that granny squares and motifs are awesome. Not only are they totally portable (yay for crocheting while commuting or waiting in line!), but they can also make really unique clothes. The key is how you connect them and how you finish them off. There is just no need for them to look like blankets wrapped on your body; in fact, I can almost guarantee you will be amazed at the gorgeous lacy fabric granny squares create when they are combined in unusual ways. Come with me now, and together we'll move beyond the afghan.

Sheryl Shawl

My mother-in-law, Sheryl, and I share a love of old movies. Whenever we are able, we turn on one of the classics and sit down to enjoy a good story. This shawl was inspired by the beautiful ball gown worn by a glamorous 1940s starlet in one of those classic films. Although the storyline has faded from my memory, the gown remains clear. This shawl captures the essence of that gown. I hope that when you wear it you will feel some of the allure that made that starlet so memorable.

Equipment

YARN: Sport-weight (#2 Fine)

Shown: Euroflax by Louet (100% Wet Spun Linen; 270 yd [247 m]/3.5 oz [100g]): willow (MC), 3 hanks. Merlin by Louet (60% Linen, 40% Merino; 250 yd [229 m]/3.5 oz [100g]): cream (CC), 1 hank.

HOOK: G/6 (4.25 mm) or hook needed to obtain gauge.

NOTIONS: Tapestry needle; straight pins or blocking pins.

GAUGE: 4 x 8″ (10.5 x 20.5 cm) = Beginning Motif.

SIZE: About 56 x 28″ (142 x 71 cm).

The Plans

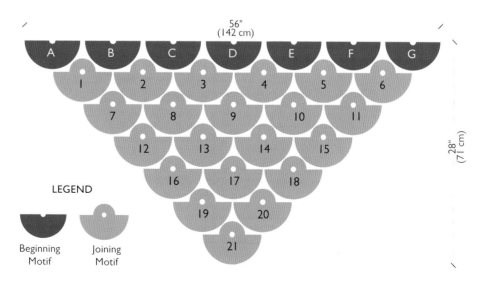

LEGEND

Beginning Motif

Joining Motif

Foundation

Beginning Motif

See stitch diagram at right for assistance.

Join 7.

With MC, ch 12, sl st to first ch (ring made).

ROW 1 (RS): Ch 3 (counts as one dc), dc in ring 16 times, turn—17 dc.

ROW 2: Ch 4 (counts as one dc and ch 1), (dc, ch 1) in each dc around to last dc, dc in last dc, turn—17 dc.

ROW 3: Ch 3 (counts as one dc), dc in each ch-1 sp and dc, fasten off, weave in ends, turn—33 dc.

ROW 4: Join CC, ch 1, sc in first dc and next 3 dc, 2 sc in next dc, [sc in next 7 dc, 2 sc in next dc] 3 times, sc in next 4 dc, fasten off, weave in ends, turn—37 sc.

ROW 5: Join MC, ch 4 (counts as one dc and ch-1 sp), [skip sc, dc in next sc, ch 1] twice, skip sc, (dc, ch 1, dc) in next sc, ch 1, *[skip sc, dc in next sc, ch 1] 3 times, skip sc, (dc, ch 1, dc) in next sc, ch 1; rep from * 3 times, [skip sc, dc in next sc, ch 1] twice, skip sc, dc in next sc, fasten off, weave in ends, turn—23 dc.

ROW 6: Join CC, ch 1, sc in each ch-1 sp and dc across, fasten off, weave in ends, turn—45 sc.

ROW 7: Join MC, ch 3 (counts as one dc), dc in next 3 sc, [2 dc in next sc, dc in next 8 sc] 4 times, 2 dc in next sc, dc in last 4 sc, turn—50 dc.

ROW 8: Ch 3 (counts as one dc), dc in next 13 dc, 2 dc in next dc, dc in next 19 dc, 2 dc in next dc, dc in rem dc, fasten off, weave in ends, turn—52 dc.

ROW 9: Join CC, ch 1, sc in each dc across, fasten off, weave in ends—52 sc.

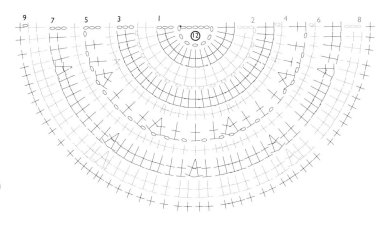

BEGINNING MOTIF

Construction

Use Plans and Legend (see p. 55) for placement of motifs. Start with motif A, working toward G. Then work Motifs 1–21.

Joining Two Beginning Motifs

Use to join Motifs A–G.

Follow directions for Beg Motif to Row 9.

ROW 9: Join CC, ch 1, sc in first dc, sl st in first sc of prev motif, sc in next dc, sl st in next sc of prev motif, cont with Row 9 above, fasten off, weave in ends.

Joining Motifs

See stitch diagram on p. 57 for assistance.

Use to join motifs 1, 7, 12, 16, 19, and 21. Create and join motifs A–G before continuing below.

With MC, ch 12, sl st to first ch (ring made).

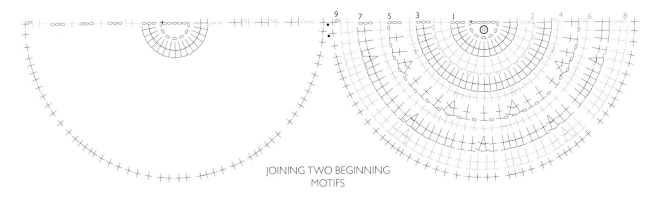

JOINING TWO BEGINNING MOTIFS

RND 1 (RS): Ch 3 (counts as one dc), 31 dc in ring, sl st to first dc, turn—32 dc.

RND 2: Ch 4 (counts as one dc and ch 1), (dc, ch 1) in each dc around, sl st to first dc, turn—32 dc.

RND 3: Ch 3 (counts as one dc), sl st in 15th sc of motif B, dc in ch-1 sp, sl st in next sc of motif B, dc in next dc, sl st in next sc of motif B, [dc in ch-1 sp, dc in next dc] 6 times, dc in ch-1 sp, sl st in 13th sc of motif A, dc in next dc, sl st in next sc of motif A, dc in ch-1 sp, sl st in next sc of motif A, [dc in next dc, dc in ch-1 sp] rep around to beginning, sl st to first dc, fasten off, weave in ends, turn—64 dc.

ROW 4: Join CC with sl st to last dc, ch 1, skip next sc of motif B, sl st to next sc of motif B, sc in next 9 dc, 2 sc in next dc, [sc in next 7 dc, 2 sc in next dc] 3 times, sc in next 9 dc, skip next sc in motif A, sl st to next sc in motif A, fasten off, weave in ends, turn—47 sc.

ROW 5: Join MC with sl st to last sc, sl st in next sc, ch 2, skip next sc in motif A, sl st to next sc in motif A, skip next sc, dc in next sc, ch 1, *[skip next sc, dc in next sc, ch 1] 3 times, skip next sc, (dc, ch 1, dc) in next sc, ch 1; rep from * 4 times, [skip next sc, dc in next sc, ch 1] 3 times, skip next sc, dc in next sc, skip next sc in motif B, sl st to next sc in motif B, ch 2, sl st to next sc, fasten off, weave in ends, turn—25 dc.

ROW 6: Join CC with sl st to last dc, ch 1, sc in next dc, sl st to next sc in motif B, sc in each ch-1 sp and dc around, sl st to next sc in motif A, fasten off, weave in ends, turn—49 sc.

ROW 7: Skip last sc, join MC with sl st to next sc, ch 2 (counts as one dc), skip next sc in motif A, sl st to next sc in motif A, dc in next 4 sc, [2 dc in next sc, dc in next 8 sc] 4 times, 2 dc in next sc, dc in last 5 sc, skip next sc in motif B, sl st to next sc in motif B, turn—52 dc.

ROW 8: Ch 2, skip next sc in motif B, sl st to next sc in motif B, skip first dc, dc in next 5 dc, [2 dc in next dc, dc in next 19 dc] twice, 2 dc in next dc, dc in next 4 dc, skip next sc in motif A, sl st to next sc in motif A, ch 2, sl st to 2nd ch of turning ch, fasten off, weave in ends, turn—53 dc.

ROW 9: Join CC with sl st to last dc, ch 1, sl st to next sc in motif A, sc in each dc around, sl st to next sc in motif B, fasten off, weave in ends—53 sc.

Joining Next Motif

Use to join remaining motifs.

Follow directions for Joining Motifs to Row 9.

ROW 9: Join CC with sl st to last dc, ch 1, sl st to next sc in motif A, sc in next dc, sl st in sc of motif 1, sc in next dc, sl st in next sc of motif 1, cont with Row 9 above, fasten off, weave in ends.

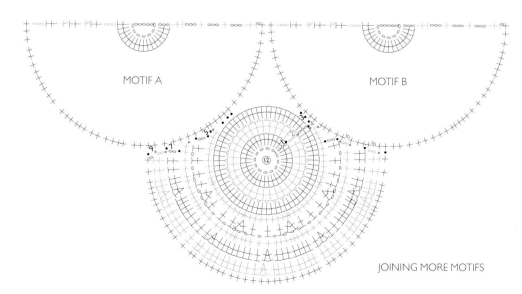

MOTIF A   MOTIF B

JOINING MORE MOTIFS

Finishing

Edging

With RS facing, join CC with sl st in any st. Ch 1, sc evenly around edge, fasten off and weave in ends.

Machine wash and put in dryer until soft. Remove from dyer when still slightly damp, lay shawl out to schematic size, pin, and allow to dry completely.

Katie Bolero

When my best friend, Katie, told me she was getting married, my brain immediately began proposing things I could crochet for her wedding. When she showed me the bridesmaids' dresses, my instant thought was, "Well, now, we need boleros to cover our shoulders." While flipping through pictures of the two of us, I was inspired by our mutual love of Gothic architecture and the beautiful stained glass windows. It only took a minute for me to add up the equation: Gothic-inspired motif plus cute little top equals the Katie Bolero.

Equipment

YARN: Worsted-weight (#4 Medium)

Shown: Oasis by South West Trading Company (100% soysilk; 240 yd [219.5 m]/ 3.5 oz [100g]): #57 Natural, 3,(3, 5, 5) hanks.

HOOKS: H/8 (5 mm) and F/5 (3.75 mm) or hooks needed to obtain gauge.

NOTIONS: Tapestry needle; blocking pins; 2 (2, 3, 3) 1 ¼" (3.2 cm) toggle buttons.

GAUGE: 4½ x 4½" (11.5 x 11.5 cm) = Granny Motif with larger hook; 4 x 4" (10.5 x 10.5 cm) = Granny Motif with smaller hook.

SIZE: Small (Medium, Large, X-Large) fits 32 (36, 40, 45)" (81.5 [91.5, 102, 114.5] cm) bust circumference and 12 (13½, 16, 18)" (30.5 [34.5, 41, 46] cm) upper arm circumference. Bolero shown in size Medium.

NOTES: *Work motifs for Small and Large sizes with smaller hook. Work Medium and X-Large sizes with larger hook. Work the first Granny Motif completely, and then join the following motifs on the last round (see Joining Two Grannies, p. 62).*

The Plans

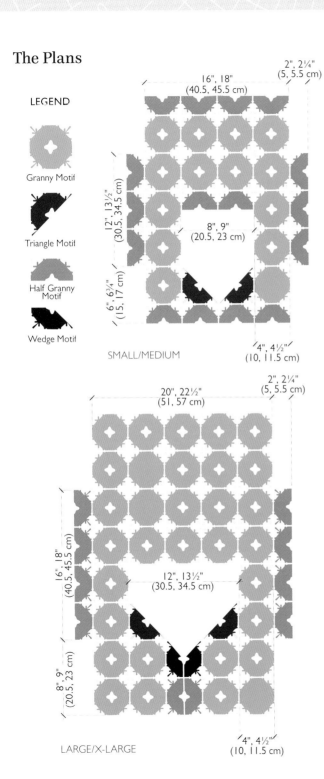

LEGEND

Granny Motif

Triangle Motif

Half Granny Motif

Wedge Motif

16", 18"
(40.5, 45.5 cm)

2", 2¼"
(5, 5.5 cm)

12", 13½"
(30.5, 34.5 cm)

8", 9"
(20.5, 23 cm)

6", 6¾"
(15, 17 cm)

4", 4½"
(10, 11.5 cm)

SMALL/MEDIUM

20", 22½"
(51, 57 cm)

2", 2¼"
(5, 5.5 cm)

16", 18"
(40.5, 45.5 cm)

12", 13½"
(30.5, 34.5 cm)

8", 9"
(20.5, 23 cm)

4", 4½"
(10, 11.5 cm)

LARGE/X-LARGE

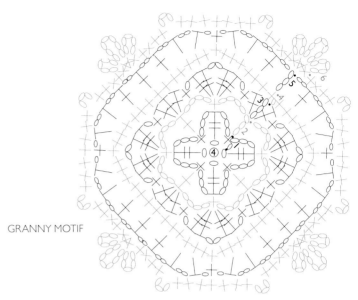

GRANNY MOTIF

Foundation

Beginning Granny Motif

Join 14, (14, 32, 32)—see Notes on p. 59.

Ch 4, sl st to first ch (ring made).

RND 1 (RS): Ch 1, [sc in ring, ch 3, tr in ring, ch 3] 4 times, sl st to sc, do not turn.

RND 2: Ch 7 (counts as dc and ch 4), [sc in next tr, ch 4, dc in next sc, ch 4] 3 times, sc in last tr, ch 4, sl st to 3rd ch of turning ch, do not turn.

RND 3: Ch 3, dc in 3rd ch, * sc in next ch-4 sp, ch 1, (2 tr, ch 2, 2 tr) in next sc, ch 1, sc in next ch-4 sp, 3 dc in next dc; rep from * around, end by sc in last ch-4 sp, dc in same ch as beg dc, sl st to 3rd ch of turning ch, do not turn.

RND 4: Ch 1, sc in turning ch of previous row, *sc in next dc, sc in next sc, sc in next ch-1 sp, sc in next 2 tr, 3 sc in next ch-2 sp, sc in next 2 tr, sc in next ch-1 sp, sc in next sc, sc in next 2 dc; rep from * around, end by sl st to first sc, do not turn.

RND 5: Ch 5, skip one sc, *dc in next sc, ch 2, skip one sc, hdc in next sc, ch 2, hdc in next sc, ch 1, skip one sc, sc in next sc, ch 1, skip one sc, hdc in next sc, ch 2, hdc in next sc, [skip one sc, ch 2, dc in next sc] twice, skip one sc, ch 2; rep from * around, end by sl st to 3rd ch of turning ch, do not turn.

RND 6: Ch 1, (sc, ch 5, sc, ch 7, sc, ch 5, sc) in turning ch (trefoil made), *2 sc in next ch-2 sp twice, ch 3, 2 sc in next ch-2 sp, sc in next ch-1 sp, sc in next sc, sc in next ch-1 sp, 2 sc in next ch-2 sp, ch 3, 2 sc in next ch-2 sp twice, (sc, ch 5, sc, ch 7, sc, ch 5, sc) in next dc; rep from * around, end with sl st in first sc, fasten off, weave in ends.

Half Granny Motif
Join 16, (16, 10, 10).

Triangle Motif
Join 2, (2, 2, 2).

Wedge Motif
Join 0, (0, 2, 2).

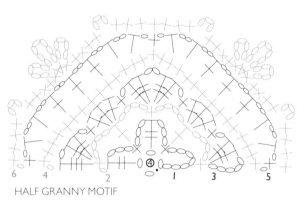

HALF GRANNY MOTIF

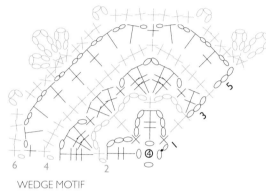

WEDGE MOTIF

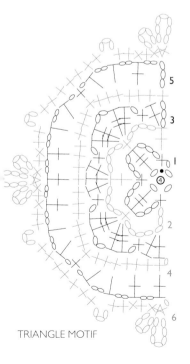

TRIANGLE MOTIF

Construction

Use Small/Medium, Large/X-Large Plans and Legend for placement of grannies.

Joining Two Grannies
Follow directions for Beginning Granny Motif on p. 60 through Rnd 5.

RND 6: Follow Rnd 6 of Beginning Granny Motif until second trefoil, (sc, ch 5, sc, ch 3, sl st to adjoining granny in ch-7 sp, ch 3, sc, ch 5, sc) in next dc, [2 sc in next ch-2 sp] twice, ch 1, sl st to adjoining granny in ch-3 sp, ch 1, sc in (next ch-2 sp and next sc of adjoining granny), sc in (same ch-2 sp and next sc of adjoining granny), sc in (next ch-1 sp and next sc of adjoining granny), sc in (next sc and sc of adjoining granny), sc in (next ch-1 sp and next sc of adjoining granny), sc in (next ch-2 sp and next sc of adjoining granny), sc in (same ch-2 sp and next sc of adjoining granny), ch 1, sl st to ch-3 sp in adjoining granny, ch 1, [2 sc in next ch-2 sp] twice, (sc, ch 5, sc, ch 3, sl st to ch-7 sp in adjoining granny, ch 3, sc, ch 5, sc) in next dc, cont with Rnd 6 of Beginning Granny Motif, fasten off, weave in ends.

JOINING TWO GRANNIES

Joining More Grannies

Join additional grannies as established in Joining Two Grannies.

JOINING MORE GRANNIES

Finishing

Lay connected motifs down, pin to schematic size, spritz with water, and allow to dry before continuing. Unwind side edges of granny squares along side seam and join side seams in same manner as above, fasten off and weave in ends.

Arm Cuff

With WS facing, join yarn with sl st and larger hook to underarm.

RND 1: Ch 1, sc evenly around opening, sl st to first sc, turn.

RND 2: Ch 1, sc in each sc around, sl st to first sc, turn.

Rep Rnd 2 twice more, fasten off, weave in ends.

Body Edging

Join yarn with sl st and larger hook to right side bottom edge of body in corner ch-7 sp.

ROW 1: Ch 1, sc in ch-7 sp, ch-6, 2 sc in sp between trefoil and ch-3 sp, 2 sc in ch-3 sp, sc in each sc, 2 sc next ch-3 sp, ch-6, sk space between ch-3 sp and trefoil, sc in ch-7 sp, continue sc evenly across body, stop when at opposite side, turn.

ROW 2: Ch 1, sc in each sc across, 5 sc in each ch-6 sp, turn.

ROW 3: Ch 1, sc in each sc across, turn.

Rep Row 3 six more times, fasten off and weave in ends.

BODY EDGING

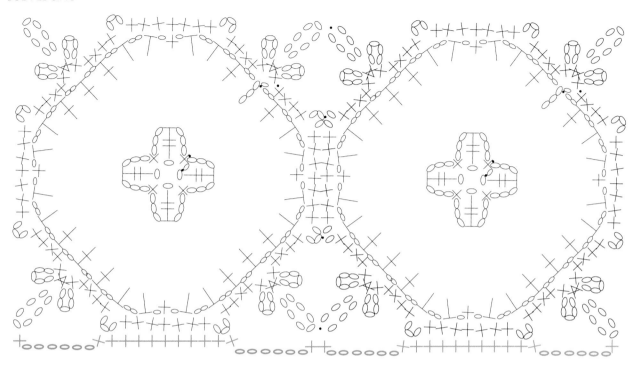

Front Body and Neck Edging

With RS facing, join yarn with sl st and larger hook to right front panel at bottom edge of body. Continue in same manner as Body Edging, working up and around neck edging through Row 4.

ROW 5: Ch 1, sc in next 6 sc, ch 2, skip 2 sc (buttonhole made), sc in next 5 sc, ch 2, skip 2 sc, (for L and XL only: sc in next 5 sc, ch 2, skip 2 sc, before continuing), sc in each sc across, turn.

ROW 6: Ch 1, sc in each sc and 2 sc in each ch-2 sp across, turn.

ROW 7: Ch 1, sc in each sc across, turn.

Rep Row 7 twice more, fasten off and weave in ends.

Sew buttons to opposite front panel side as buttonholes with yarn and needle.

Megan Sweater

My niece, Megan, and I share a love of car coats, our favorite sweaters to wear during the cold winter months. No matter whether we are running out to get the paper or just a bit chilly at work, we both reach for our car coats. This sweater was born from that love, coupled with my adoration of granny squares. I hope this project gives you a warm feeling while you crochet it, but beware, you will love this sweater so much you will soon be wearing it everywhere you go!

Equipment

YARN: **DK-weight (#3 Light)**

Shown: Swirl DK by Lorna's Laces (85% merino wool, 15% silk; 150 yd [137.5 m]/ 1.75 oz [50g]): poppy, 10 (11, 14, 16) hanks.

HOOKS: G/6 (4.25 mm) and H/8 (5 mm) or hooks needed to obtain gauge.

NOTIONS: Tapestry needle; blocking pins; sewing needle and thread.

Optional: 4″ (10 cm) of ½″ (1.3 cm)-wide grosgrain ribbon; 1 hook and eye closure.

GAUGE: 3½ x 3½″ (9 x 9 cm) = Granny Square with smaller hook;

$3^{7}/_{8}$ x $3^{7}/_{8}$″ (10 x 10 cm) = Granny Square with larger hook.

SIZE: Small (Medium, Large, X-Large) fits 30 (33, 40, 44)″ (76.5 [84, 102, 112] cm) bust circumerence and 15 (16¼, 20, 22)″ (38.5 [42, 51, 56] cm) upper arm circumference.

Sweater is shown in Medium.

> NOTES: *Work motifs for Small and Large sizes with smaller hook.*
> *Work Medium and X-Large sizes with larger hook.*

The Plans

LEGEND

Granny Square

Joining Motif

Half Granny Square

¾ Granny Square

Half Joining Motif

Small Granny

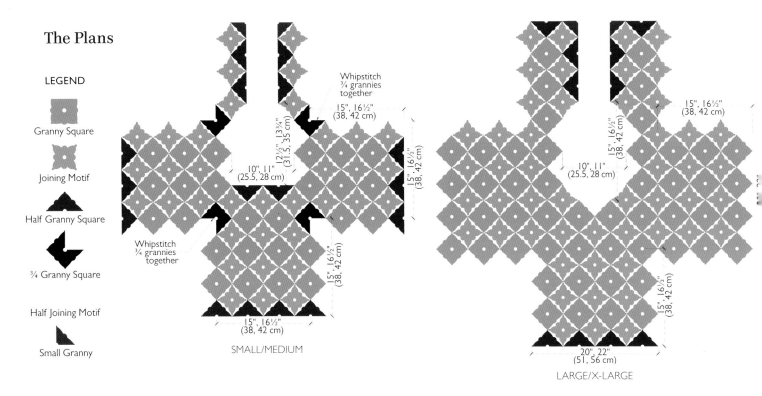

Whipstitch ¾ grannies together

15", 16½" (38, 42 cm)

16½" (38, 42 cm)

10", 11" (25.5, 28 cm)

12½" 13¾" (31.5, 35 cm)

15", 16½" (38, 42 cm)

Whipstitch ¾ grannies together

15", 16½" (38, 42 cm)

SMALL/MEDIUM

15", 16½" (38, 42 cm)

15", 16½" (38, 42 cm)

10", 11" (25.5, 28 cm)

15", 16½" (38, 42 cm)

20", 22" (51, 56 cm)

LARGE/X-LARGE

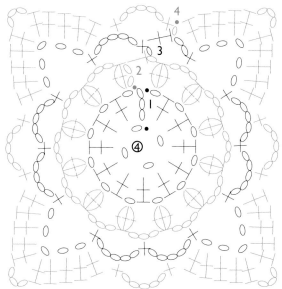

GRANNY SQUARE MOTIF

Foundation

Granny Square Motif

Join 26 (26, 50, 50).

Ch 4, sl st to first ch (ring made).

RND 1 (RS): Ch 4 (counts as one dc + ch-1 sp), (dc, ch 1) in ring 11 times, sl st to 3rd ch of tch, do not turn.

RND 2: Sl st in first ch-1 sp, ch 2, dc2tog in same ch-1 sp, *ch 3, skip dc, dc-cl in next ch-1 sp; rep from * around, ch 1, hdc to dc2tog, do not turn.

RND 3: Ch 1, sc around post of hdc, *ch 5, sc in next ch-3 sp; rep from * around, ch 2, dc in first sc, do not turn.

RND 4: Ch 1, sc around post of dc, [ch 5, sc in next ch-5 sp, (5 dc, ch 3, 5 dc) in next ch-5 sp, sc in next ch-5 sp] 3 times, ch 5, sc in next ch-5 sp, (5 dc, ch 3, 5 dc) in next ch-5 sp, sl st to first sc, fasten off, weave in ends.

Half Granny Square
Join 16 (16, 10, 10).

Small Granny
Join 2 (2, 2, 2).

¾ Granny
Join 4 (4, 0, 0).

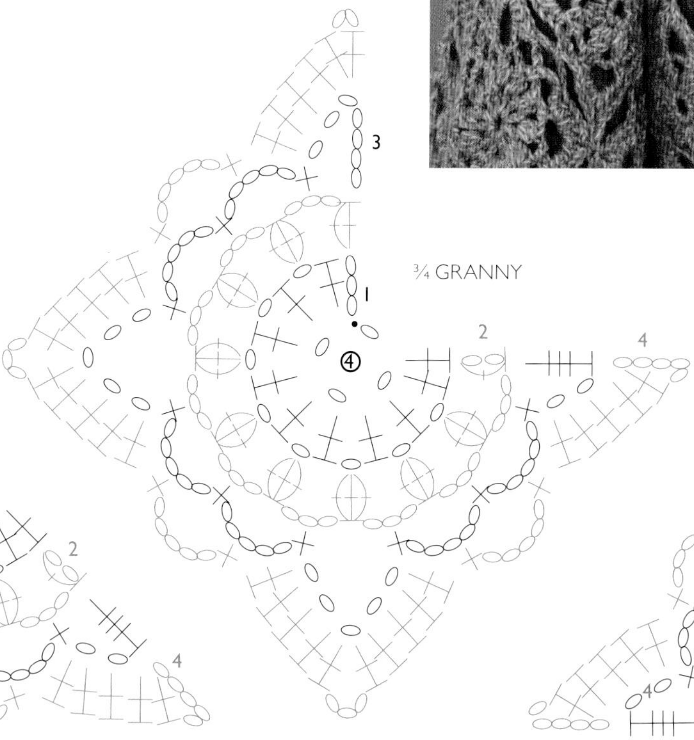

¾ GRANNY

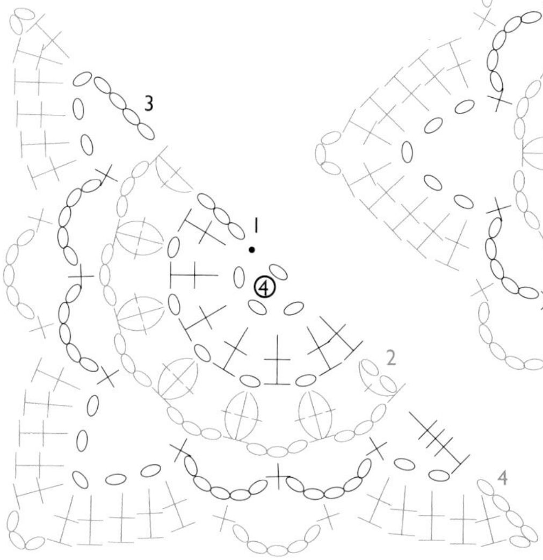

HALF GRANNY SQUARE

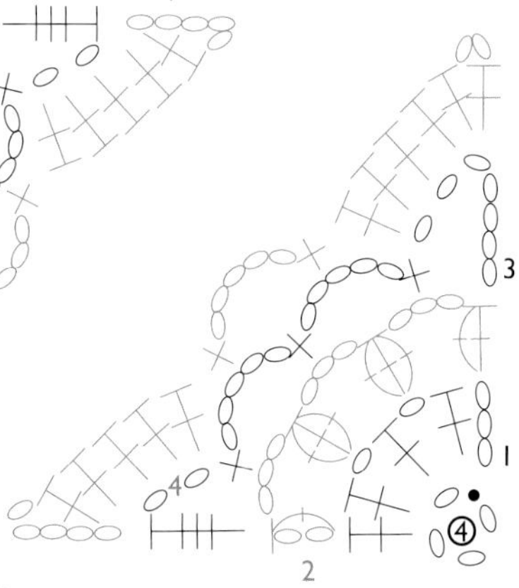

SMALL GRANNY

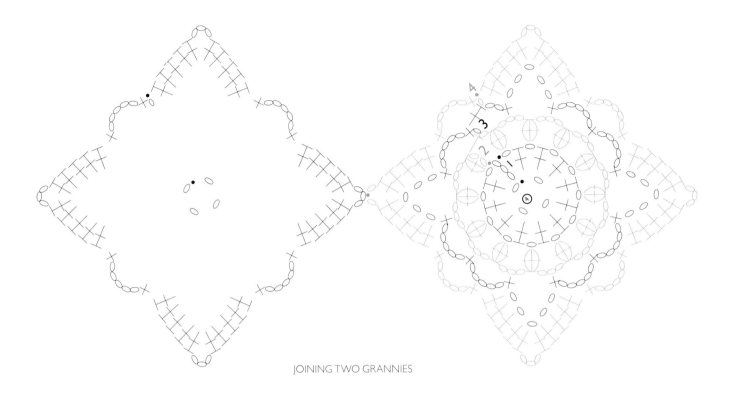

JOINING TWO GRANNIES

Construction

Use Small/Medium, Large/X-Large Plans and Legend for place-ment of grannies and joining motifs. Do not weave in ends at sleeve or side edges until after you block and join the seams.

Joining Two Grannies

Follow directions for Granny Square Motif on p. 68 to Rnd 3.
Rnd 4: Follow Rnd 4 of Granny Square Motif to 2nd ch-5 sp, 5 dc in ch-5 sp, ch 1, sl st to adjoining granny's ch-3 sp, ch 1, 5 dc in same ch-5 sp, cont with Rnd 4 of Granny Square Motif, fasten off, weave in ends.

Joining More Grannies

Follow directions for Joining Two Grannies; continue in same manner by connecting all corner ch-3 sps.

JOINING MORE GRANNIES

JOINING MOTIF

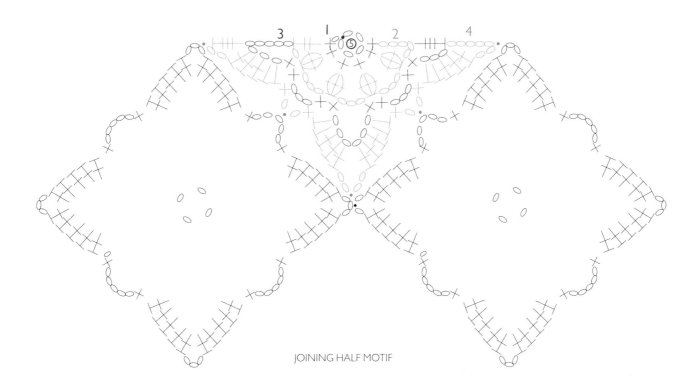

JOINING HALF MOTIF

Joining Motif

Ch 5, sl st to first ch (ring made).

RND 1 (RS): Ch 1, sc in ring 8 times total, sl st to first sc, do not turn.

RND 2: Ch 2, dc2tog in first sc, *(ch 3, dc-cl) in next sc; rep from * around, ch 3, sl st to dc2tog, do not turn.

RND 3: Ch 1, *(sc, ch 3, sc) in next ch-3 sp, (sc, ch 6, sc) in next ch-3 sp; rep from * around, sl st to first sc, do not turn.

RND 4: Ch 1, *sc in ch-3 sp, ch 1, sl st to adjoining granny's ch-5 sp, ch 1, sc in same ch-3 sp, (2 hdc, 3 dc, ch 2, sl st to adjoining granny's ch-3 sp, ch 2, 3 dc, 2 hdc) in next ch-6 sp; rep from * around, sl st to first sc, fasten off, weave in ends.

Joining Half Motif

Follow directions for Joining Motif, continuing in the same manner and connecting all ch-sps.

Finishing

Lay connected motifs down, pin to schematic size, spritz with water, and allow to dry before continuing. Fold sweater in half widthwise, aligning side seams and sleeve edges. Unwind side seam edges to join grannies. Connect side and sleeve seams in same manner as above, fasten off, and weave in ends. (S and M only): With tapestry needle and yarn, whipstitch underarm ¾ grannies together.

Arm Cuff and Body Edging

Join yarn with smaller hook to sleeve seam or bottom body edge with RS facing, ch 15.

ROW 1: Sc in 2nd ch from hook and ea ch across, sl st to fabric twice (first sl st joins ribbing to motifs, second counts as a tch), turn—14 sc.

ROW 2: Skip both sl sts, sc-blp in ea sc across, turn.

ROW 3: Ch 1, sc-blp in ea sc across, sl st to fabric twice, turn.

ROWS 4–6: Rep Rows 2–3, ending with Row 2.

ROW 7: Ch 3, dc-blp in ea sc across, sl st to fabric twice, turn.
Arm cuffs only: Rep Rows 2–7 evenly around opening. Fasten off. Arm Cuffs only: Sew ends of cuffs together with whipstitch. Weave in ends.

Neck Edging

See stitch diagram at right for assistance.

Join yarn with sl st and same hook as motifs to right side of joining motif at front corner edge of neck, 2 sc in first ch-2 sp of joining motif, sc in next 2 dc, ch 4, skip (dc, 2 hdc, sc), 2 sc in next ch-3 sp, ch 4, skip (sc, 2 hdc, dc), sc in next 2 dc, 2 sc in ch-2 sp, sl st to corner, fasten off, weave in ends. This straightens the edge at the neck. Rep for each joining motif along neck.

Front Edging

Join yarn with smaller hook to right side bottom edge of body edging. Follow directions for Body Edging, fasten off, weave in ends.

Hook and Eye (optional)

Cut grosgrain ribbon in half. Fold edges down, pin one half to WS of front edging at waist, sew in place. Pin other half to opposite front edging, sew in place. Sew hook to first half, sew eye to second half.

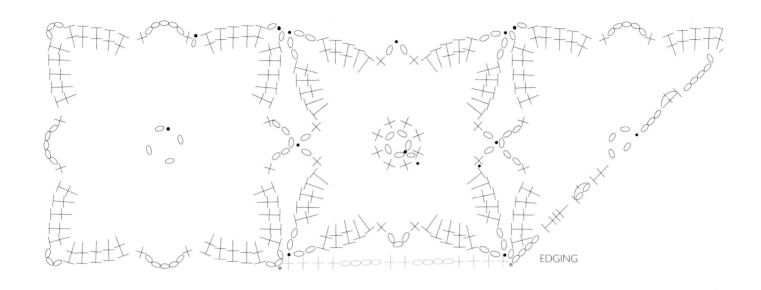

EDGING

Belt Loops (optional)

Make 4. With smaller hook, ch 12.

ROW 1: Sl st in 2nd ch from hook and ea ch across, turn—11 sl st.

ROW 2: Working in opposite side of ch, sl st in ea ch across, fasten off, leave long tail for sewing. Sew belts loops to waist at quarter points using long tails and tapestry needle.

Belt (optional)

With smaller hook, ch 10.

ROW 1: Sc in 2nd ch from hook and ea ch across, turn—9 sc.

ROW 2: Ch 1, sc in ea sc across, turn.

Repeat Row 2 until belt measures 50 (53, 60, 64)" (127 [135, 152.5, 162.5] cm) from beginning, fasten off, weave in ends.

Maggie Wrap Top

My niece, Maggie, is über stylish, in such a special way. She doesn't rely on labels, but always finds great bargains and knows how to wear a new outfit to make herself shine. Last time we were together, probably doing nothing more then eating lunch, this design sprang into my mind. I just knew it would make the perfect addition to the long top and gaucho pants she was wearing. Since the top is worked in all granny motifs, you can easily personalize it by leaving off the motifs at the arms for a cap sleeve look or by adding more motifs to the body for a kimono look.

Equipment

YARN: DK-weight (#3 Light)

Shown: Love by South West Trading Company and Vickie Howell Collection

(70% bamboo, 30% silk; 98 yd [90 m]/ 1.75 oz [50 g]): #248 jack and sally, 11 (13, 15, 17) hanks.

HOOKS: H/8 (5 mm) and I/9 (5.5 mm) or hooks needed to obtain gauge.

NOTIONS: Tapestry needle; $7/8''$ (2.2 cm) button; hook and eye closure; $4''$ (10.5 cm) of $5/8''$ (1.5 cm) wide grosgrain ribbon; blocking pins; small sewing needle; matching thread.

GAUGE: $4\frac{1}{4}$ x $4\frac{1}{4}''$ (11 x 11 cm) = Granny Motif with smaller hook;

$4\frac{3}{4}$ x $4\frac{3}{4}''$ (12 x 12 cm) = Granny Motif with larger hook.

SIZE: Small (Medium, Large, X-Large) fits 34 (38, 42 $\frac{1}{2}$, 47 $\frac{1}{2}$)" (86.5 [96.5, 108, 120.5] cm) bust circumference and $12\frac{3}{4}$ ($14\frac{1}{4}$, 17, 19)" (32.5 [36.5, 43.5, 48.5] cm) upper arm circumference.

Top shown in size Small.

NOTES: *Work motifs for Small and Large sizes with smaller hook.*
Work motifs for Medium and X-Large sizes with larger hook.

The Plans

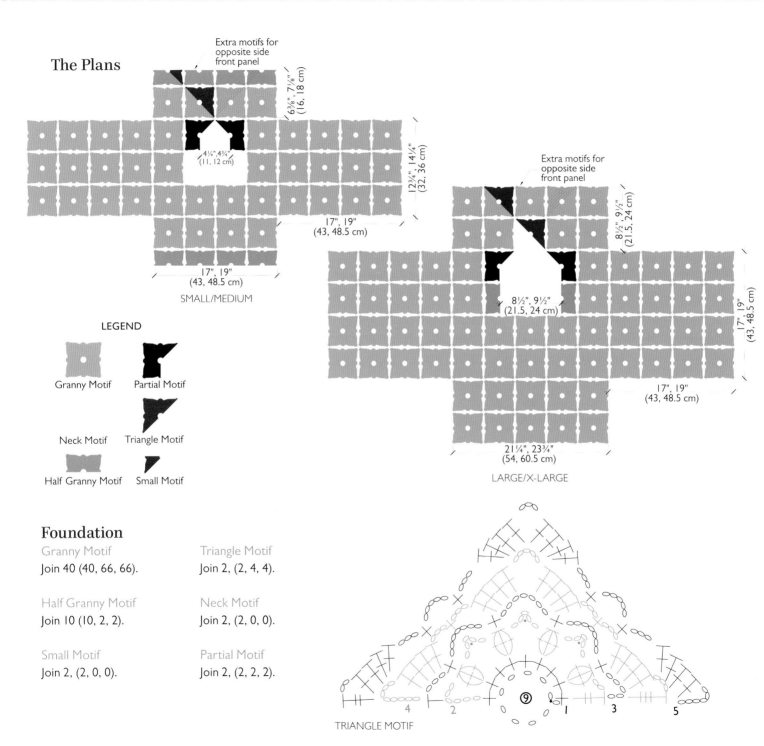

Extra motifs for opposite side front panel

6³⁄₈", 7⅛" (16, 18 cm)

4¼", 4¾" (11, 12 cm)

12¾", 14¼" (32, 36 cm)

17", 19" (43, 48.5 cm)

17", 19" (43, 48.5 cm)

SMALL/MEDIUM

Extra motifs for opposite side front panel

8½", 9½" (21.5, 24 cm)

8½", 9½" (21.5, 24 cm)

17", 19" (43, 48.5 cm)

21¼", 23¾" (54, 60.5 cm)

LARGE/X-LARGE

LEGEND

Granny Motif

Partial Motif

Neck Motif

Triangle Motif

Half Granny Motif

Small Motif

Foundation

Granny Motif
Join 40 (40, 66, 66).

Triangle Motif
Join 2, (2, 4, 4).

Half Granny Motif
Join 10 (10, 2, 2).

Neck Motif
Join 2, (2, 0, 0).

Small Motif
Join 2, (2, 0, 0).

Partial Motif
Join 2, (2, 2, 2).

4   2   ⑨   I   3   5

TRIANGLE MOTIF

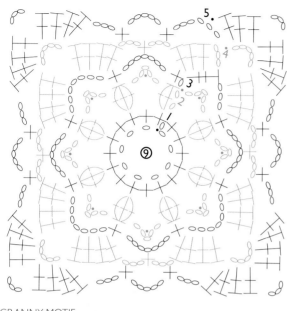

GRANNY MOTIF

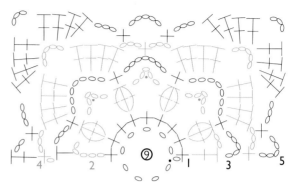

HALF GRANNY MOTIF

SMALL MOTIF

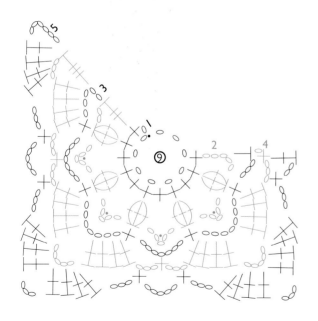

PARTIAL MOTIF

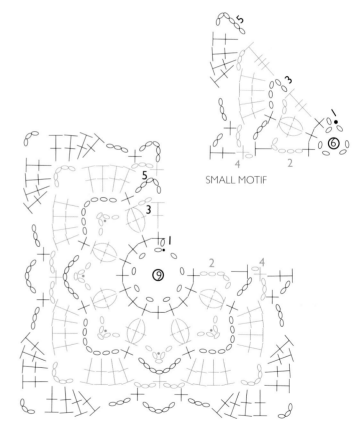

NECK MOTIF

Construction

Joining Two Grannies

Follow stitch diagram at left.

Joining More Grannies

Follow stitch diagram at right.

JOINING TWO GRANNIES

JOINING MORE GRANNIES

ARM CUFF

Finishing

Lay connected motifs down, pin to schematic size, spritz with water, and allow to dry before continuing. Unwind side edges of granny squares along side seam and connect side and sleeve seams in same manner as Joining More Grannies, fasten off, and weave in ends.

Neck Edging

With RS facing, join yarn with sl st to right front panel at bottom edge of body. Ch 1, sc evenly around neck opening, fasten off and weave in ends.

Arm Cuff

With RS facing, join yarn with sl st to seam side of cuff at a motif corner.

RND 1: Ch 1, 2 sc in ch-3 sp, work (sc in each of next 4 dc, ch 2, sk ch-3 sp, 3 sc in ch-5 sp, ch 2, sk ch-3 sp, sc in ea of next 4 dc, 2 sc in next ch-3 sp, sc in ch-1 sp) across each motif around, sl st to first sc, turn.

RND 2: Ch 1, sc in each sc across, 2 sc in ea ch-2 sp, turn.

RND 3: Ch 1, sc in ea sc around, sl st to first sc, turn.

Rep Rnd 2 three more times, fasten off, weave in ends.

Body Edging

With RS facing, join yarn with sl st to front left panel at
bottom edge of body.

(S, M ONLY) ROW 1: Ch 1, sc evenly across bottom of body,
 stop when at opposite side, turn.

ROW 2: Ch 1, sc in each sc across, turn.

(L, XL ONLY) ROW 1: Follow Rnd 1 of arm edging, do not sl st
 to beginning, turn.

ROW 2: Ch 1, sc in each sc across, 2 sc in ea ch-2 sp, turn.

(ALL SIZES) ROW 3: Ch 1, sc in each sc across, turn.

ROW 4: Ch 1, sc in each of next 3 sc, ch 3, skip 3 sc
 (buttonhole made), sc in each sc across, turn.

ROW 5: Ch 1, sc in ea sc across, 3 sc in ch-3 sp, turn.

ROW 6: Ch 1, sc in ea sc across, turn.

Rep Row 6 once, fasten off, weave in ends.

Wrap right front panel across left front panel to place the
button using the buttonhole as a guide. Sew button with
yarn and needle.

Cut ribbon in half, fold edges under. Sew one piece to left front
panel on opposite end of button. Sew the second piece to the
wrong side of right front panel opposite the first ribbon. Sew
hook and eye to ribbon pieces with needle and matching thread.

Paige Sweetheart Top

My niece, Paige, is one of those people you just want to spend the whole afternoon talking and daydreaming with. This light and breezy top, with its delicate lace and romantic construction, reminds me of some of those afternoons. The motifs are easy once you have mastered the repeats, but the combination of motifs will have all your admirers wondering how you dreamed up such a beautiful top.

Equipment

YARN: DK-weight (#3 Light)

Shown: Bamboo by South West Trading Company

(100% bamboo; 250 yd [229 m]/ 3.5 oz [100 g]): #402 magenta, 4 (5, 5, 6) hanks.

HOOKS: G/6 (4.25 mm) and H/8 (5 mm) or hooks needed to obtain gauge.

NOTIONS: Tapestry needle; 6 (6, 8, 8) ⁵⁄₁₆″ (8 mm) pearl buttons;
blocking pins; small needle and matching thread.

GAUGE: 5½ x 5½″ (14 x 14 cm) = Granny Motif with smaller hook;
6 x 6″ (15 x 15 cm) = Granny Motif with larger hook.

SIZE: Small (Medium, Large, X-Large) fits 33 (36, 44, 48)″ (84 [91.5, 112, 122] cm)
bust circumference, and 11 (12, 16½, 18)″ (28 [30.5, 42, 45.5] cm) upper arm circumference.
Top shown in size Small.

NOTES: *Work motifs for Small and Large sizes with smaller hook.*
Work motifs for Medium and X-Large sizes with larger hook.

The Plans

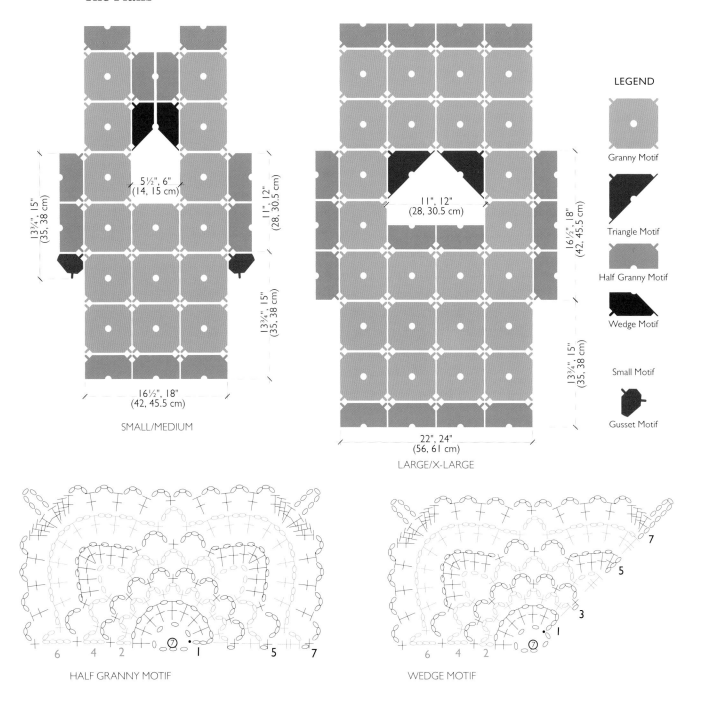

5½", 6"
(14, 15 cm)

13¾", 15"
(35, 38 cm)

1 1", 12"
(28, 30.5 cm)

13¾", 15"
(35, 38 cm)

16½", 18"
(42, 45.5 cm)

SMALL/MEDIUM

11", 12"
(28, 30.5 cm)

16½", 18"
(42, 45.5 cm)

13¾", 15"
(35, 38 cm)

22", 24"
(56, 61 cm)

LARGE/X-LARGE

LEGEND

Granny Motif

Triangle Motif

Half Granny Motif

Wedge Motif

Small Motif

Gusset Motif

HALF GRANNY MOTIF

6 4 2 0 ⑦ 1 5 7

WEDGE MOTIF

6 4 2 ⑦ 1 3 5 7

Foundation

Granny Motif
Join 15 (15, 24, 24).

Half Granny Motif
Join 11 (11, 16, 16).

Triangle Motif
Join 0 (0, 2, 2).

Wedge Motif
Join 2 (2, 0, 0).

GRANNY MOTIF

TRIANGLE MOTIF

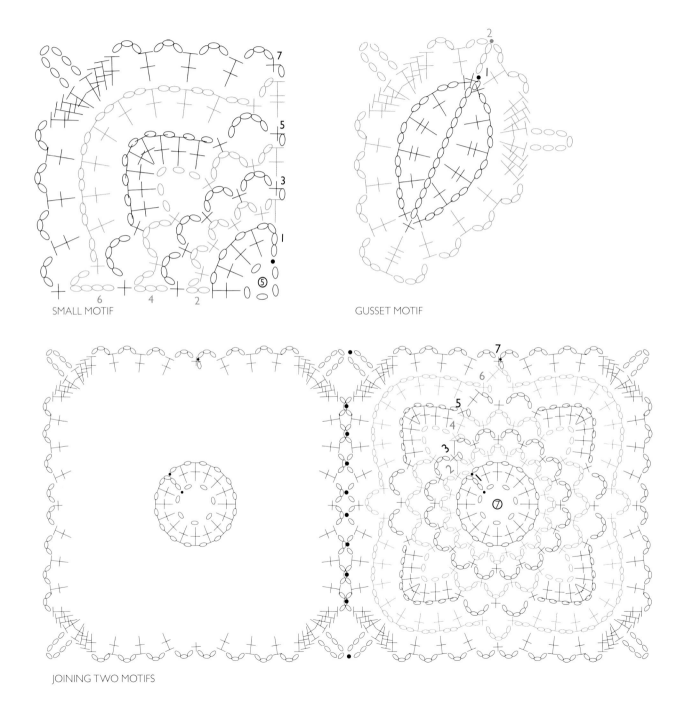

SMALL MOTIF

GUSSET MOTIF

JOINING TWO MOTIFS

Small Motif
Join 2 (2, 0, 0).

Gusset Motif
Join 2 (2, 0, 0).

Construction
Use Small/Medium, Large/X-Large Plan and Legend
for placement of grannies.

Joining Two Motifs
Follow stitch diagram for Joining Two Motifs on
last round.

Joining Half Granny Motifs
Follow stitch diagram for Joining Half Granny Motifs
on last round.

Joining More Motifs
See diagram on p. 90.

JOINING HALF GRANNY MOTIFS

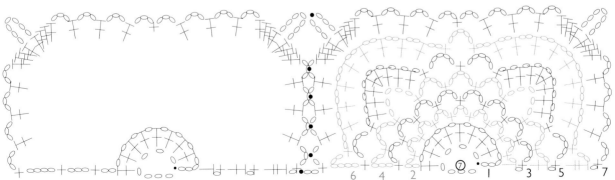

JOINING MORE MOTIFS

Finishing

Lay connected motifs down, pin to schematic size, spritz with water, and allow to dry before continuing. Unwind side edges of granny squares along side seam and connect side seams by following diagrams for joining motifs, fasten off, and weave in ends.

Arm Cuff

With WS facing, join yarn with sl st to underarm at any corner st.
RND 1: Ch 1, sc evenly around, sl st to first sc, turn.
RND 2: Ch 1, *sc in next sc, ch 3, sc in next sc; rep from * around, sl st to first sc, fasten off, weave in ends.

Body Edging

With WS facing, join yarn with sl st to corner st at bottom edge of front right panel.
ROW 1: Ch 1, sc evenly across bottom edge, turn.
ROWS 2–3: Ch 1, sc in ea sc across, turn.
ROW 4: Ch 1, *sc in next sc, ch 3, sc in next sc; rep from * across, fasten off, weave in ends.

Neck Edging

See Neck Edging diagram for assistance.
With WS facing, join yarn with sl st to corner st at bottom edge of front left panel.
ROW 1: Ch 1, sc evenly up and around panel and neck body, at corners of motifs ch 4, sc in ch-7 sp, sc in sl st, sc in ch-7 sp, ch 4, cont sc evenly, stop when at corner of opposite side edge, turn.
ROW 2: Ch 1, sc in each sc and ch across, turn.
ROW 3: Ch 1, [sc in next 9 sc, ch 1, skip 1 sc (buttonhole made)] 6 (6, 8, 8) times, sc in each sc across, turn.
ROW 4: Ch 1, working in sc and ch: *sc in next st, ch 3, sc in next st; rep from * around, fasten off, weave in ends.
With needle and thread, sew buttons to opposite front panel side using buttonholes as a guide.

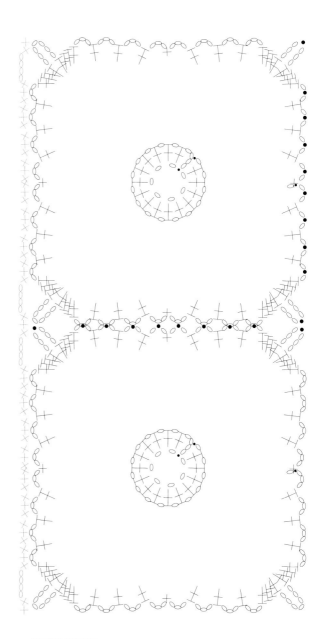

NECK EDGING

Raeanne Shawl Sweater

My niece, Raeanne, and I have found that we both have days when we feel like we have two different personalities battling it out to decide what to wear. One wants to wear all comfortable baggy clothes, and the other wants to wear the latest fashion. This sweater was designed for days like that. It's easy to wear and makes you feel nice and snuggly, while the big shawl collar gives you the look of the most current runway model. Pin the fronts up high for a more structured look, or leave the front flaps open for a relaxed, breezy look.

Equipment

YARN: Sport-weight (#2 Fine)

Shown: Chelsea by Lily Chin Signature Collection

(30% Merino Wool, 35% Cotton, 35% Acrylic; 191 yd [174.5 m]/1.75 oz [50 g]):

#5811 light blue, 7 (9, 11, 13) balls.

HOOKS: H/8 (5 mm) and G/6 (4.25 mm) or hooks needed to obtain gauge.

NOTIONS: Tapestry needle; blocking pins; 4 (4, 5, 5) ³⁄₈″ (1 cm) black pearl buttons; sewing needle and thread.

GAUGE: 3¼ x 3¼″ (8.5 x 8.5 cm) = Granny Motif with smaller hook; 3⅝″ x 3⅝″ (9.5 x 9.5 cm) = Granny Motif with larger hook.

SIZE: Small (Medium, Large, X-Large) fits 34 (38, 40, 44)″ (86.5 [96.5, 102, 112] cm) bust circumference. Finished bust measures 32½″ (36¼″, 39″, 43½″) (82.5 [92, 99, 110.5] cm). Sweater is shown in size Small.

NOTES: *Work motifs for Small and Large sizes with smaller hook.*
Work motifs for Medium and X-Large sizes with larger hook.

The Plans

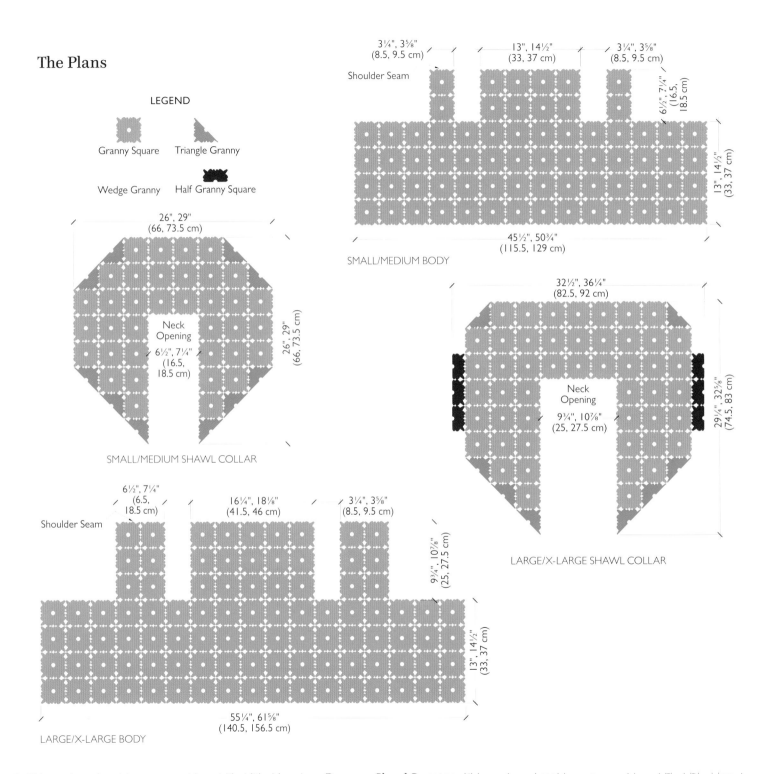

LEGEND

Granny Square

Triangle Granny

Wedge Granny

Half Granny Square

SMALL/MEDIUM SHAWL COLLAR

26", 29"
(66, 73.5 cm)

26", 29"
(66, 73.5 cm)

Neck Opening
6½", 7¼"
(16.5, 18.5 cm)

SMALL/MEDIUM BODY

3¼", 3⅝"
(8.5, 9.5 cm)

13", 14½"
(33, 37 cm)

3¼", 3⅝"
(8.5, 9.5 cm)

6½", 7¼"
(16.5, 18.5 cm)

13", 14½"
(33, 37 cm)

45½", 50¾"
(115.5, 129 cm)

Shoulder Seam

LARGE/X-LARGE SHAWL COLLAR

32½", 36¼"
(82.5, 92 cm)

29¼", 32⅝"
(74.5, 83 cm)

Neck Opening
9¾", 10⅞"
(25, 27.5 cm)

LARGE/X-LARGE BODY

6½", 7¼"
(6.5, 18.5 cm)

16¼", 18⅛"
(41.5, 46 cm)

3¼", 3⅝"
(8.5, 9.5 cm)

Shoulder Seam

9¾", 10⅞"
(25, 27.5 cm)

13", 14½"
(33, 37 cm)

55¼", 61⅝"
(140.5, 156.5 cm)

Foundation

Granny Square Motif
Join 104 (104, 144, 144).

Triangle Motif
Join 10 (10, 8, 8).

Half Granny Motif
Join 0 (0, 6, 6).

Wedge Motif
Join 0 (0, 4, 4).

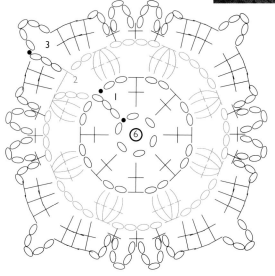

GRANNY SQUARE MOTIF

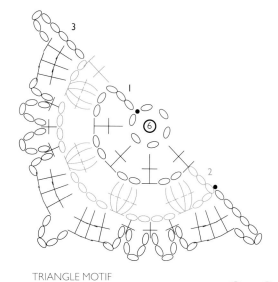

TRIANGLE MOTIF

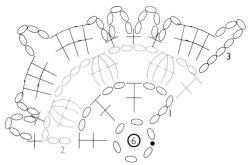

HALF GRANNY MOTIF

WEDGE MOTIF

JOINING TWO GRANNIES

Construction

Use Small/Medium, Large/X-Large Plan and Legend for placement of grannies for both the body and the shawl collar. Do not
weave in ends on the shawl collar at the neck edge and do not
weave in ends on the body at the shoulder edge.

Joining Two Grannies
Follow stitch diagram at left.

Joining More Grannies
Follow stitch diagram at right.

JOINING MORE GRANNIES

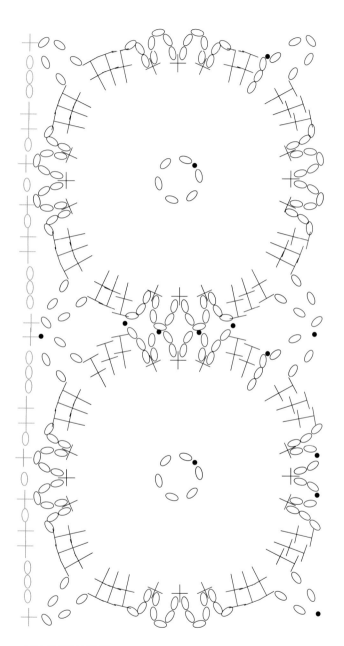

ARM CUFF EDGING

Finishing

Lay connected motifs down for both body and shawl collar, pin to schematic size, spritz with water, and allow to dry before continuing. Unwind side edges of motifs along shoulder seam and join shoulder seams as for joining motifs above, fasten off, and weave in ends.

Attach shawl collar to body: Line up center 2 (2, 3, 3) motifs on neck opening of collar with center 2 (2, 3, 3) motifs on back neck of body and pin. Working out from center, line up each motif with motifs on shoulder and neck edges of body, ending with a triangle motif on the upper corner motif on each front panel. Join shawl collar to body as for Joining Two Grannies on p. 96, fasten off, weave in ends.

Arm Cuff Edging
See stitch diagram at left for assistance.
With RS facing, join yarn with sl st in corner ch-5 sp of underarm motif.
RND 1: Ch 1, [sc in ch-5 sp, ch 3, skip 2 dc, sc in next dc, sc in next ch-3 sp, (ch 1, sc in next ch-5 sp) twice, ch 1, sc in next ch-3 sp, sc in next dc, skip 2 dc, ch 3, sc in next ch-5 sp] rep across ea granny square around, sl st to first sc.
RND 2: Ch 1, sc evenly around opening, sl st to first sc, fasten off, weave in ends.

Shawl Collar Edging
With WS facing, join yarn with sl st in corner ch-5 sp at end of collar.
ROW 1: Ch 1, for ea granny square edge: [sc in ch-5 sp, ch 3, skip 2 dc, sc in next dc, sc in next ch-3 sp, (ch 1, sc in next ch-5 sp) twice, ch 1, sc in next ch-3 sp, sc in next dc, skip 2 dc, ch 3, sc in next ch-5 sp], sc evenly across all triangle, half, and wedge grannies, turn.
ROW 2: Ch 1, sc evenly across, fasten off, weave in ends.

Body Edging

Lay sweater flat with front facing up and wrap one front panel over the other 14⅝ (16¼, 17⅞, 20)" (37 [41.5, 45.5, 51] cm) from end or to desired hip measurement. (Note: Using granny squares as a guide, wrap panels until grannies align). Pin front panels together. Join yarn with sl st to right side bottom edge of body at a corner ch-5 sp.

RND 1: Working through both layers of front, ch 1, [sc in ch-5 sp, ch 3, skip 2 dc, sc in next dc, sc in next ch-3 sp, (ch 1, sc in next ch-5 sp) twice, ch 1, sc in next ch-3 sp, sc in next dc, skip 2 dc, ch 3, sc in next ch-5 sp] rep on ea granny square around, sl st to first sc, turn.

ROW 2: Ch 16, sc in 2nd ch from hook and each ch across, sl st to body twice (first sl st joins ribbing to body, second counts as a turning ch), turn—15 sc.

ROW 3: Ch 1, sc-blp in each sc across, turn.

ROW 4: Ch1, sc-blp in ea sc across, sl st twice to body, turn.

Rep Rows 3–4 evenly around body, fasten off, weave in ends. With tapestry needle, whipstitch ribbing seams together.

Sew buttons to front panel side with yarn and needle, spacing them equally along ribbing.

✳ Stitch Pattern Styles

Crochet stitches can make the most unique and exciting fabric out there, don't you agree? There's only a handful of stitches, yet they can make thousands of different patterns just by varying how you use that hook. In this chapter, you will delve deeply into exploring the uniqueness of crochet fabric. You will play with combining texture and drape, lacy fabric, and structure. You will use stitch patterns that are simple, yet striking in garments. Here you are going to find details that you have not been able to see before, all because of crochet symbols. Step inside to see the great surprises in store for you.

Sarah Bee Dress

As soon as the first flower starts to pop its tiny head out of the ground, my niece, Sarah, wants to pack all her winter clothes away and break into her summer dresses. But since spring can be cold, I decided it was time to crochet her a dress that could be worn over her lighter summer dresses so she won't freeze. The wool/linen blend keeps you warm, yet is light enough to layer. The tiny bees in the stitch pattern will remind you of spring each time you wear the dress.

Equipment

YARN: Sport-weight (#2 Fine)

Shown: Louet MerLin (60% Linen, 40% Merino; 250 yd [229 m]/3.5 oz [100 g]):

#60 goldilocks, 6 (7, 8, 9) hanks.

HOOK: G/6 (4.25 mm) or hook needed to obtain gauge.

NOTIONS: Tapestry needle; stitch markers; blocking pins and spray bottle; one 12″ (30.5 cm) for S or M, or 14″ (35.5 cm) for L or XL, matching invisible zipper; matching sewing thread and sewing needle;

Optional: 3 (3, 4, 4) yards of ½″ (1.5 cm)-wide grosgrain ribbon.

GAUGE: 20 st (2 SR) by 12 rows (3 SR) = 4 x 4.25″ (10.5 x 11 cm) in Honey Bee Stitch Pattern; 19 sc by 24 rows = 4 x 4″ (10.5 x 10.5 cm) in SC.

SIZE: Small (Medium, Large, X-Large) fits 34 (38, 42, 46)″ (86.5 [96.5, 106.5, 117] cm) bust circumference.

Dress shown in size Small.

NOTES: *Garment is crocheted from the top down in one piece.*
Garment is worked in rows to the hips, then joined and worked in rounds to the end.

The Plans

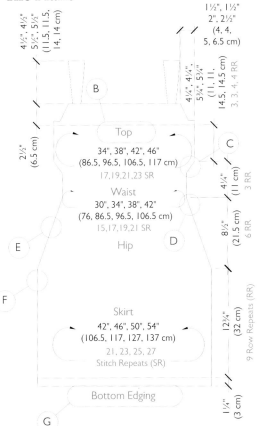

A. HONEY BEE STITCH PATTERN (HBSP)

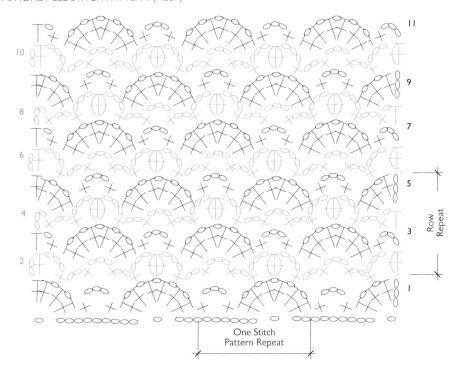

One Stitch Pattern Repeat

Foundation

Special Stitches

SHELL: (DC, CH1) 5 TIMES IN ST, DC IN SAME ST
HALF SHELL: (DC, CH1) TWICE IN ST, 2DC IN SAME ST

Honey Bee Stitch Pattern (HBSP)

See stitch diagram A for assistance. Ch 34.

ROW 1: ([Dc, ch 1] twice, dc) in 4th ch from hook (turning ch counts as one dc), *skip 3 ch, sc in next ch, ch 3, skip one ch, sc in next ch, skip 3 ch, shell in next ch; rep from * across to last 10 ch, skip 3 ch, sc in next ch, ch 3, skip one ch, sc in next ch, skip 3 ch, half shell in last ch, turn—2 shells and 2 half shells, 3 SR.

ROW 2 (RS): Ch 2, dc in first dc, ch 3, sc in next ch-1 sp, ch 2, skip next ch-1 sp, (sc, ch 3, sc) in ch-3 sp, *ch 2, skip next ch-1 sp, sc in next ch-1 sp, ch 3, dc-cl in next ch-1 sp, ch 3, sc in next ch-1 sp, ch 2, skip next ch-1 sp, (sc, ch 3, sc) in ch-3 sp; rep from * across to last ch-3 sp, ch 2, skip next ch-1 sp, sc in next ch-1 sp, ch 3, dc2tog in last dc, turn.

ROW 3: Ch 3, skip dc2tog, sc in ch-3 sp, skip ch-2 sp, shell in ch-3 sp, *skip ch-2 sp, sc in ch-3 sp, ch 3, skip dc-cl, sc in ch-3 sp, skip ch-2 sp, shell in ch-3 sp; rep from * across to last ch-2 sp, skip ch-2 sp, sc in ch-3 sp, ch 1, hdc in last dc, turn—3 shells, 3 SR.

ROW 4: Ch 3, sc in ch-1 sp, ch 2, skip ch-1 sp, sc in next ch-1 sp, ch 3, dc-cl in next ch-1 sp, ch 3, sc in next ch-1 sp, *ch 2, skip next ch-1 sp, (sc, ch 3, sc) in ch-3 sp, ch 2, skip next ch-1 sp, sc in next ch-1 sp, ch 3, dc-cl in next ch-1 sp, ch 3, sc in next ch-1 sp; rep from * across to last ch-1 sp, ch 2, skip last ch-1 sp, (sc, ch 1, hdc) in last ch-3 sp, turn.

ROW 5: Ch 3 (counts as one dc), ([dc, ch 1] twice, dc) in ch-1 sp, *skip ch-2 sp, sc in ch-3 sp, ch 3, skip dc-cl, sc in next ch-3 sp, skip ch-2 sp, shell in next ch-3 sp; rep from * to last dc-cl, skip ch-2 sp, sc in ch-3 sp, ch 3, skip last dc-cl, sc in next ch-3 sp, skip ch-2 sp, half shell in last ch-3 sp, turn—2 shells and 2 half shells, 3 SR.

Rep Rows 2–5 to desired length.

Construction

Top

See stitch diagram B for assistance.

Ch 174 (194, 214, 234).

ROW 1 (WS): Follow Row 1 of HBSP—16 (18, 20, 22) shells and 2 half shells, 17 (19, 21, 23) SR.

Rep Rows 2–5 of HBSP 3 (3, 4, 4) times—3 (3, 4, 4) RR.

B. TOP

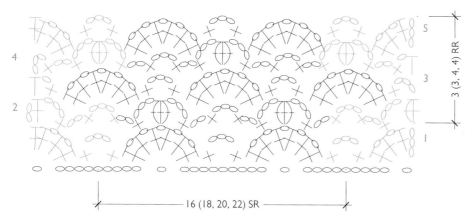

C. BUST SHAPING

5

3

1

4

2

Bust Shaping

See stitch diagram C for assistance on decrease.

ROW 1: Follow Row 2 of HBSP to second dc-cl, *ch 3, sc in next ch-1 sp, ch 2, skip next ch-1 sp, sc in ch-3 sp (decrease made), pm in sc just made, ch 2, skip next ch-1 sp, sc in next ch-1 sp, ch 3, dc-cl in next ch-1 sp*, cont in Row 2 of HBSP for 3 (4, 5, 6) more dc-cl, rep between * * once, cont in Row 2 of HBSP to end, turn.

ROW 2: Follow Row 3 of HBSP across, working (dc, ch 1, dc) in each marked sc (move pm to ch-1 sp made), turn—15 (17, 19, 21) shells, 15 (17, 19, 21) SR.

ROW 3: Follow Row 4 of HBSP to ch-3 sp before pm, *(sc, ch 3, sc) in ch-3 sp, ch 1 (move pm to ch-1 sp), skip (dc, ch 1, dc), (sc, ch 3, sc) in next ch-3 sp*, cont in Row 4 of HBSP to ch-3 sp before next pm, rep between * * once, cont in Row 4 of HBSP to end, turn.

ROW 4: Follow Row 5 of HBSP to ch-3 sp before pm, *(dc, ch 1, dc, ch 1, dc) in ch-3 sp, tr in ch-1 sp (move pm to tr just made), (dc, ch 1, dc, ch 1, dc) in next ch-3 sp*, cont in Row 5 of HBSP to ch-3 sp before next m, rep between * * once, cont in Row 5 of HBSP to end, turn—13, 15, 17, 19 shells and 6 half shells.

ROW 5: Follow Row 2 of HBSP to first tr (pm), *ch 3, dc-cl in tr, ch 3, sc in next ch-1 sp*, cont in Row 2 of HBSP to next tr (pm), rep between * * once, cont in Row 2 of HBSP to end, turn.

Waist

Rep Rows 3–5 of HBSP once, rep Rows 2–5 of HBSP once—2 RR.

Waist Shaping and Joining

See stitch diagram D for assistance on increase.

ROW 1: Ch 2, dc in first dc, *ch 3, sc in next ch-1 sp, ch 2, skip next ch-1 sp, (sc, ch 5, sc) in ch-3 sp (increase made)*, cont in Row 2 of HBSP for 7 (8, 9, 10) dc-cl, rep between * * once, cont in HBSP to end, turn.

ROW 2: Follow Row 3 of HBSP to ch-5 sp, *([dc, ch 1] 7 times, dc) in ch-5 sp (extra large shell made)*, cont in HBSP to next ch-5 sp, repeat between * * once, cont in HBSP to end, turn—13 (15, 17, 19) shells and 2 extra large shells, 15 (17, 19, 21) SR.

ROW 3: Follow Row 4 of HBSP to first extra large shell, *ch 2, skip first ch-1 sp on shell, [sc in next ch-1 sp, ch 3, dc-cl in next ch-1 sp, ch 3] twice, sc in next ch-1 sp, ch 2, skip next ch-1 sp*, cont in HBSP to next extra large shell, rep between * * once, cont in HBSP to end, turn.

ROW 4: Follow Row 5 of HBSP to double dc-cl on extra large shell, *sc in first ch-3 sp, ch 3, skip first dc-cl, sc in next ch-3 sp, ch

D. WAIST SHAPING

3, sc in next ch-3 sp, ch 3, skip second dc-cl, sc in next ch-3 sp (increase made)*, cont in HBSP to next double dc-cl on extra large shell, rep between * * once, cont in HBSP to end, turn.

ROW 5: Follow Row 2 of HBSP to first increase, *(sc, ch 3, sc) in first ch-3 sp, (ch 2, sc, ch 3, dc-cl, ch 3, sc, ch 2) in next ch-3 sp, (sc, ch 3, sc) in next ch-3 sp*, cont in HBSP to next increase, rep between * * once, cont in HBSP to end, turn.

Rep Rows 3–4 of HBSP once.

ROW 8: Follow Row 5 of HBSP to last half shell, (dc, ch 1, dc, ch 1, dc) in last ch-3 sp, sl st to tch at beginning of Row 8 to join work, turn (note: work will now be crocheted in turned rounds instead of rows).

Hip Shaping and Skirt

See stitch diagram E for assistance on joining rounds. See stitch diagram F (p. 108) for working in rounds.

RND 1: Ch 2, dc2tog in tch, *ch 3, sc in next ch-1 sp, ch 2, skip next ch-1 sp, (sc, ch 5, sc) in ch-3 sp (increase made)*, cont in Row 2 of HBSP for 8 (9, 10, 11) dc-cl, rep between * * once, cont in HBSP to end, sl st to dc2tog, turn.

RND 2: Ch 1, sc in ch-3 sp, cont in Row 3 of HBSP to increase (ch-5 sp), *([dc, ch 1] 7 times, dc) in ch-5 sp (extra large shell made)*, cont in HBSP to next ch-5 sp, rep between * * once,

sc in next ch-3 sp, dc in first sc, turn—15 (17, 19, 21) shells and 2 extra large shells, 17 (19, 21, 23) SR.

RND 3: Ch 1, sc in dc, *ch 2, skip next ch-1 sp, [sc in next ch-1 sp, ch 3, dc-cl in next ch-1 sp, ch 3] twice, sc in next ch-1 sp, ch 2, skip next ch-1 sp*, cont in Row 4 of HBSP to next extra large shell, rep between * * once, cont in HBSP to end, sc around dc (into dc-sp), ch 1, hdc to first sc, turn.

RND 4: Ch 4, (dc, ch 1, dc) in ch-1 sp, cont in Row 5 of HBSP to double dc-cl on extra large shell, *sc in first ch-3 sp, ch 3, skip first dc-cl, sc in next ch-3 sp, ch 3, sc in next ch-3 sp, ch 3, skip second dc-cl, sc in next ch-3 sp (increase made)*, cont in HBSP to next double dc-cl on extra large shell, rep between * * once, [dc, ch 1] 3 times in ch-1/hdc-sp, sl st to 3rd ch of beg ch 4, turn.

E. JOINING ROWS

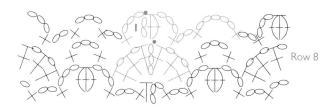

Row 8

F. WORKING IN ROUNDS

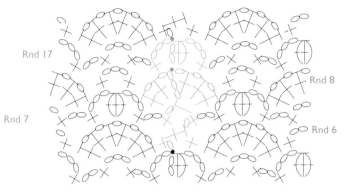

Rnd 17

Rnd 8

Rnd 7

Rnd 6

RND 5: Ch 2, dc2tog in first dc, cont in Row 2 of HBSP to first increase, *(sc, ch 3, sc) in first ch-3 sp, (ch 2, sc, ch 3, dc-cl, ch 3, sc, ch 2) in next ch-3 sp, (sc, ch 3, sc) in next ch-3 sp*, cont in HBSP to next increase, rep between * * once, cont in HBSP to end, sl st to dc2tog, turn.

RND 6: Ch 1, sc in ch-3 sp, cont in Row 3 of HBSP around to first dc2tog, sc in ch-3 sp, dc in first sc, turn—19 (21, 23, 25) shells, 19 (21, 23, 25) SR.

RND 7: Ch 1, sc in dc, cont in Row 4 of HBSP around to last dc, sc around dc (into dc-sp), ch 1, hdc to first sc, turn.

RND 8: Ch 4 (counts as one dc and ch 1), (dc, ch 1, dc) in ch-1 sp, cont in Row 5 of HBSP around, [dc, ch 1] 3 times in ch-1/hdc-sp, sl st to 3rd ch of beg ch 4, turn.

Rep Rnd 1 above except place increase 9 (10, 11, 12) dc-cl apart.

Rep Rnds 2–8 above.

RND 17: Ch 2, dc2tog in first dc, cont in Row 2 of HBSP around, sl st to dc2tog, turn.

Rep Rnds 6–8 above once.

Rep last 4 rnds 7 more times, turn.

Rep Rnds 17 and 6 once more, turn.

Bottom Edging

See stitch diagram G for assistance on bottom edging.

RND 1: Ch 1, sc around dc (into dc-sp), *skip sc, skip (dc, ch 1), [sc in next dc, sc in ch-1 sp] 3 times, sc in next dc, skip (ch 1, dc), skip sc, 3 sc in ch-3 sp*; rep between * * around to first dc-sp, 2 sc around dc (into dc-sp), sl st to first sc, turn.

RND 2: Ch 1, sc in each sc around, sl st to first sc, turn.

Rep Rnd 2 five more times, fasten off, weave in ends.

Top Edging

Back

ROW 1: With RS facing, join yarn in first ch of foundation edge with sl st, ch 1, sc evenly across row, turn.

ROWS 2–3: Ch 1, sc in each sc across, turn—171 (191, 211, 231) sc.

ROW 4: Sl st in next 3 (3, 5, 8) sc, ch 1, sc in each sc for 79 (89, 95, 99) sc, leave remain sts unworked, turn.

ROWS 5–6: Ch 1, sc in each sc across, turn.

ROW 7: Ch 1, sc2tog over first 2 sc, sc in each sc across to last 2 sc, sc2tog over last 2 sc, turn.

ROW 8: Ch 1, sc in each st across, turn.

ROW 9: Ch 1, sc in each sc across, turn.

Rep Rows 7–9 twice, rep Row 7 once more, fasten off, weave in ends.

Front

ROW 1: Skip 6 (6, 10, 16) sc from end of Row 4, join yarn with sl st, ch 1, sc in each sc across to last 3 (3, 5, 8) sc, leave remaining sts unworked, turn.

Rep Rows 5–16, fasten off, weave in ends.

Straps

First Strap

ROW 1: Join yarn to WS front 2 sc from end with sc, sc in next 4 sc, turn—5 sc.

ROW 2: Ch 1, sc in each sc across, turn.

Rep Row 2 three times.

ROW 6: Ch 1, sc in first 2 sc, 2 sc in next sc, sc in last 2 sc, turn—6 sc.

Rep Row 2 five times.

G. BOTTOM EDGING

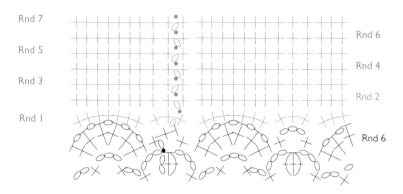

Rnd 7
Rnd 5
Rnd 3
Rnd 1

Rnd 6
Rnd 4
Rnd 2
Rnd 6

ROW 12: Ch 1, sc in first 3 sc, 2 sc in next sc, sc in last 2 sc, turn—7 sc.
Rep Row 2 five times.
ROW 18: Ch 1, sc in first 3 sc, 2 sc in next sc, sc in last 3 sc, turn—8 sc.
Rep Row 2 five times.
ROW 24: Ch 1, sc in first 4 sc, 2 sc in next sc, sc in last 3 sc, turn—9 sc.
Rep Row 2 six (six, eighteen, eighteen) times.
ROW 31 (31, 43, 43): Ch 1, sc in first 4 sc, sc2tog over next 2 sc, sc in last 3 sc, turn—8 sc.
Rep Row 2 five times.
ROW 37 (37, 49, 49): Ch 1, sc in first 3 sc, sc2tog over next 2 sc, sc in last 3 sc, turn—7 sc.
Rep Row 2 five times.
ROW 43 (43, 55, 55): Ch 1, sc in first 3 sc, sc2tog over next 2 sc, sc in last 2 sc, turn—6 sc.
Rep Row 2 five times.
ROW 49 (49, 61, 61): Ch 1, sc in first 2 sc, sc2tog over next 2 sc, sc in last 2 sc, turn—5 sc.
Rep Row 2 four times.
Pin strap 2 sc from back edge with RS facing, sl st thru both strap and back in each sc across, turn, fasten off, weave in ends.

Second Strap
ROW 1: Join yarn to WS front 7 sc from end with sc, sc in next 4 sc, leave remaining 2 sc unworked, turn—5 sc.
Beginning with Row 2, work as for First Strap, fasten off, weave in ends.

Finishing
Zipper Seam
Join yarn with sl st to right side of top side seam. Sc evenly around opening, fasten off, weave in ends.

Wash and dry dress in washing machine and dryer to desired softness. Pin dress to schematic size. Spritz with water, and allow to dry. Pin zipper to WS of side opening. With matching thread and sewing needle, sew zipper to dress.

Strengthen Straps (optional)
To strengthen straps, pin grosgrain to wrong side of each strap, backstitch in place with sewing thread and needle. Pin remaining ribbon to wrong side along the top edge of dress (be sure to cover ribbon on straps). Fold ends under. Backstitch to top with sewing thread and needle.

Rachel Swing Jacket

The '60s-inspired swing jacket has over taken my sketchbook, and nearly every jacket I draw has the same boxy lines with flaring sleeves. I knew I had to create one soon, but I had been quite hesitant to do so, because they don't usually flatter a figure with any curves. After talking with my niece, Rachel, I realized that a cross between her super-trendy style and my classic lines would be just the ticket. In that spirit, you can decide whether you want the jacket to swing or to show off your curves by moving the back bands one button over to cinch in the waist.

Equipment

YARN: Sport-weight (#2 Fine)

Shown: Louet Gems Sportweight (100% Merino Wool; 225 yd [206 m] / 3.5 oz [100 g]):
#11 cherry red (MC), 6 (7, 8, 9) hanks; #62 citrus orange (CC), 1 (1, 1, 1) hank.

HOOK: F/5 (3.75 mm) or hook needed to obtain gauge.

NOTIONS: Tapestry needle; stitch markers; two size 4 snap closures; twelve ¾" (2 cm) round buttons, 28" (71.5 cm) of ¾" (2 cm)-wide grosgrain ribbon; matching sewing thread and needle; blocking pins.

Optional: 32 (32, 36, 36)" (81.5 [81.5, 91.5, 91.5] cm) of ¾" (2 cm)-wide grosgrain ribbon for neck lining;

GAUGE: 24 st (6 SR) by 16 rows (8 RR) = 4 x 4⅛" (10 x 10.5 cm) in Brick Stitch Pattern.

SIZE: Small (Medium, Large, X-Large) fits 31 (35, 39, 42)" (79 [89, 99, 107] cm) bust circumference.
Top shown in size Small.

> NOTE: *Jacket is worked in the round from the top down.*

The Plans

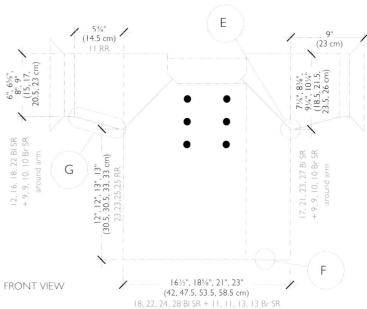

FRONT VIEW

5¾"
(14.5 cm)
11 RR

6", 6⅝"
8", 9"
(15, 17,
20.5, 23 cm)
around arm

12, 16, 18, 22 Bl SR
+ 9, 9, 10, 10 Br SR

E

9"
(23 cm)

7¼", 8⅜"
9¼", 10¼"
(18.5, 21.5,
23.5, 26 cm)
around arm

17, 21, 23, 27 Bl SR
+ 9, 9, 10, 10 Br SR

G

12", 12", 13", 13"
(30.5, 30.5, 33, 33 cm)
23, 23, 25, 25 RR

F

16½", 18⅝", 21", 23"
(42, 47.5, 53.5, 58.5 cm)
18, 22, 24, 28 Bl SR + 11, 11, 13, 13 Br SR

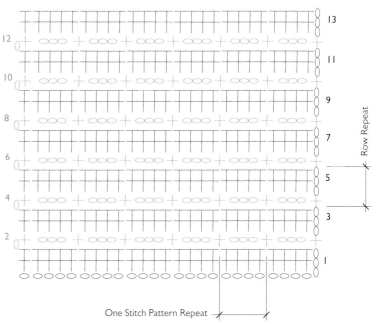

12
10
8
6
4
2

13
11
9
7
5
3
1

Row Repeat

One Stitch Pattern Repeat

A. BRICK STITCH PATTERN (BRSP)

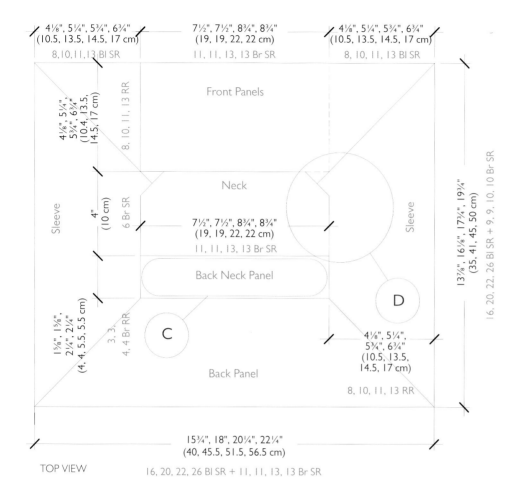

4⅛", 5¼", 5¾", 6¾"
(10.5, 13.5, 14.5, 17 cm)
8, 10, 11, 13 Bl SR

7½", 7½", 8¾", 8¾"
(19, 19, 22, 22 cm)
11, 11, 13, 13 Br SR

4⅛", 5¼", 5¾", 6¾"
(10.5, 13.5, 14.5, 17 cm)
8, 10, 11, 13 Bl SR

Front Panels

4⅛", 5¼", 5¾", 6¾"
(10.4, 13.5, 14.5, 17 cm)

8, 10, 11, 13 RR

Neck

Sleeve

4" (10 cm)

6 Br SR

7½", 7½", 8¾", 8¾"
(19, 19, 22, 22 cm)
11, 11, 13, 13 Br SR

Sleeve

13⅞", 16⅛", 17¾", 19¾"
(35, 41, 45, 50 cm)

16, 20, 22, 26 Bl SR + 9, 9, 10, 10 Br SR

Back Neck Panel

D

1⅝", 1⅝", 2¼", 2¼"
(4, 4, 5.5, 5.5 cm)

3, 3,
4, 4 Br RR

C

4⅛", 5¼",
5¾", 6¾"
(10.5, 13.5,
14.5, 17 cm)
8, 10, 11, 13 RR

Back Panel

15¾", 18", 20¼", 22¼"
(40, 45.5, 51.5, 56.5 cm)

TOP VIEW

16, 20, 22, 26 Bl SR + 11, 11, 13, 13 Br SR

Foundation

Brick Stitch Pattern (BrSP)

See stitch diagram A for assistance. Ch 28.

ROW 1 (RS): Dc in 4th ch from hook, dc in ea ch across to end,
turn—25 dc; 6 SR.

ROW 2: Ch 1, sc in dc, *ch 3, skip 3 dc, sc in between next 2 dc;
rep from * to last 4 dc, ch 3, sc in tch, turn.

ROW 3: Ch 3, *skip sc, 4 dc in ch-3 sp; rep from * across, dc in last
sc, turn.

Rep Rows 2–3 to desired length.

Block Stitch Pattern (BISP)

See stitch diagram B for assistance. Ch 22.

ROW 1 (RS): Dc in 4th ch from hook, dc in ea ch across to end, turn—19 dc; 6 SR.

ROW 2: Ch 1, sc in dc, *ch 2, skip 2 dc, sc in between next 2 dc; rep from * to last 3 dc, ch 2, sc in tch, turn.

ROW 3: Ch 3, *skip sc, 3 dc in ch-2 sp*; rep from * across, dc in last sc, turn.

Rep Rows 2–3 to desired length.

Construction

Back Neck Panel

With MC, ch 48 (48, 56, 56).

ROWS 1–6 (6, 8, 8): Working in BrSP, crochet back neck panel as shown in diagram C—11 (11, 13, 13) SR. Fasten off, weave in ends.

Neck

See stitch diagram D for assistance on forming front, back, and sleeve panels.

With MC, join yarn with sl st to beginning row of back neck panel left side. Ch 27 (to form top of sleeve), dc3tog in 5th, 6th, and 7th ch from hook, ch 41 (41, 49, 49) (to form front panel), fasten off. Rep on opposite side of back neck, do not fasten off.

ROW 1 (RS): Ch 2, cont in BrSP to dc3tog, 4 dc in sp along side of dc3tog, 4 dc in corner ch, 4 dc in other side (working in ch before bottom of dc3tog and in each ch of dc3tog), cont in BrSP to back neck panel, 4 dc around post of ea dc along back neck panel edge, 4 dc in corner sc, cont in BrSP across back neck, 4 dc in next corner sc, 4 dc around post of ea dc on opposite back neck panel edge, cont in BrSP across ch to dc3tog, 4 dc on bottom edge of dc3tog, 4 dc in corner ch, 4 dc in sp on other side of dc3tog, cont in BrSP to end, turn.

ROW 2: Follow BrSP to ea corner 4-dc, (ch 2, skip one dc, sc between next 2 dc, ch 2, sc in same sp, ch 2, skip one dc, sc between next 2 dc) in ea corner 4-dc, turn.

B. BLOCK STITCH PATTERN (BISP)

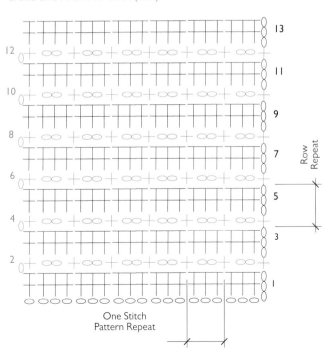

One Stitch
Pattern Repeat

Row Repeat

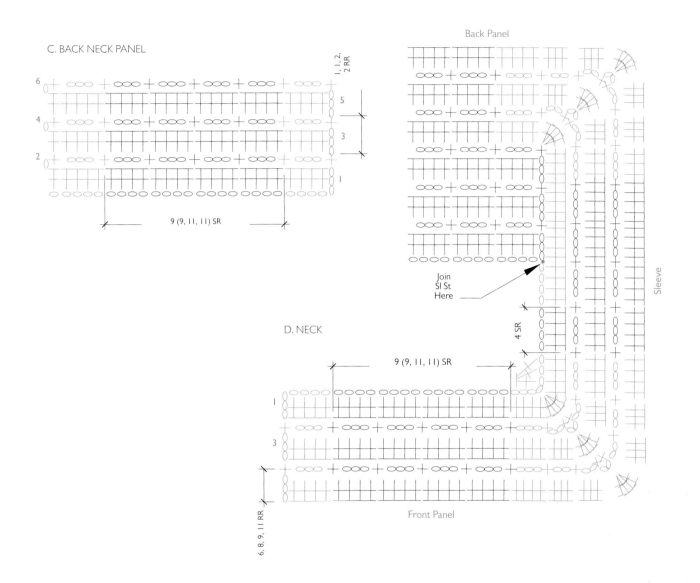

C. BACK NECK PANEL

1, 1, 2, 2 RR

6
5
4
3
2
1

9 (9, 11, 11) SR

Back Panel

Join
Sl St
Here

Sleeve

D. NECK

9 (9, 11, 11) SR

4 SR

1
3

6, 8, 9, 11 RR

Front Panel

E. JOINING BODY

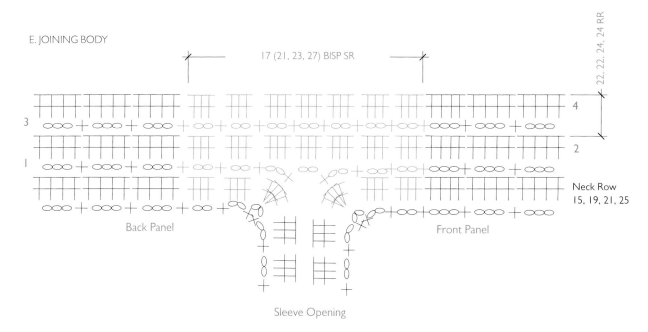

17 (21, 23, 27) BISP SR

22, 22, 24, 24 RR

Neck Row
15, 19, 21, 25

Back Panel

Front Panel

Sleeve Opening

ROW 3: Follow BrSP in all ch-3 sps, follow BISP in all ch-2 sps, 4 dc in corner ch-2 sps, turn.

ROWS 4–15 (19, 21, 25): Using BrSP and BISP, cont as shown in diagram D, do not fasten off. Lay top down, pin to schematic size (see top view), spritz with water, and allow to dry.

Body

Fold top in half, matching front to back. Begin working in rows around body, and ignoring the sleeves.

See stitch diagram E for assistance on joining front and back panels.

ROW 1 (WS): Cont in BrSP and BISP to first 4-dc corner on front panel, *ch 2, skip one dc, sc between next 2 dc, ch 2, skip over to next 4-dc corner on back panel, skip one dc, sc between next 2 dc, ch 2*, cont in BISP and BrSP to next 4-dc corner, repeat between * *, cont in BISP and BrSP to end, turn—34 (42, 46, 54) BISP; 33 (33, 39, 39) BrSP.

Cont in stitch pattern for 23 (23, 25, 25) RR from join.

ROW 47 (47, 51, 51): Ch 1, sc in first dc, *skip one dc, sc in next 2 dc, sc between next 2 dc; rep from * across BrSP, *skip one dc, sc in next dc, sc between next 2 dc*; rep between * * across BISP, cont to end, turn (see stitch diagram F for assistance).

EDGING RND: Ch 1, sc in ea sc across bottom of body to last sc, 3 sc in last sc, turn 90 degrees, sc evenly up body opening to neck, 3 sc in first ch, *skip one ch, sc in next 2 ch, sc between next 2 ch, rep from * across neck to last ch, 3 sc in last ch, turn 90 degrees, sc evenly down body opening, 2 sc in same st as first sc, sl st to first sc to join, fasten off, weave in ends.

Sleeves

Begin working in turned rounds around sleeve, and decreasing one SR every 4 rounds. Repeat directions for ea sleeve. See stitch diagram G (p. 117) for assistance.

With WS facing, join MC with sl st to center of 4 dc corner on front panel.

RND 1: Ch 1, sc in same sp, cont in BISP and BrSP around sleeve to next 4-dc corner on back panel, sc in center of 4-dc group, ch 2, sl st to first sc to join, turn—17 (21, 23, 27) BISP; 9 (9, 10, 10) BrSP.

RND 2: Sl st in first ch-2 sp, ch 3 (counts as one dc), 2 dc in same ch-2 sp, cont in BISP and BrSP around, sl st to 3rd ch of tch to join, turn.

RND 3: Ch 1, sc between tch and next dc, ch 2, sk 2 ch, sc between next 2 dc, cont in BISP and BrSP around to last 3-dc group, ch 1, sl st to first sc to join, turn.

RND 4: Sl st in first ch-1 sp, ch 3 (counts as dc), 3 dc in next ch-2 sp, cont in BISP and BrSP around, sl st to 3rd ch of tch, turn—16 (20, 22, 26) BISP; 9 (9, 10, 10) BrSP.

RND 5: Ch 1, sc between tch and next dc, cont in BISP and BrSP around to tch, sc between last dc and tch, sl st to first sc, turn.

RND 6: Sl st in first sc, sl st in next ch-2 sp, ch 3 (counts as one dc), 2 dc in same ch-2 sp, cont in BISP and BrSP around, sl st to 3rd ch of tch to join, turn.

RND 7: Ch 1, sc between tch and next dc, ch 1, skip one dc, sc between next 2 dc, ch 2, cont in BISP and BrSP around, ch 2, sl st to first sc, turn.

RND 8: Sl st in first ch-2 sp, ch 3 (counts as one dc), 2 dc in ch-2 sp, cont in BISP and BrSP around to ch-1 sp, dc in ch-1 sp, sl st to 3rd ch of tch to join, turn—15 (19, 21, 25) BISP; 9 (9, 10, 10) BrSP.

RND 9: Ch 1, sc between tch and next dc, sc between same dc and next dc, ch 2, cont in BISP and BrSP around, ch 2, sl st to first sc to join, turn.

Rep Rnds 2–9 once, then rep Rnds 2–6 once—12 (16, 18, 22) BISP; 9 (9, 10, 10) BrSP.

RND 23: Ch 1, sc between tch and next dc, *skip next dc, sc in next dc, sc between next 2 dc; rep from * across BISP, **skip one dc, sc in next 2 dc, sc between next 2 dc; rep from ** across BrSP, cont to end, sl st to first sc, turn—51 (59, 66, 74) sc.

RND 24: Ch 1, sc in ea sc around, sl st to first sc to join, turn.

Repeat Rnd 24 six more times.

RND 31: Ch 3 (counts as one dc), dc in first sc, 2 dc in ea sc around, sl st in 3rd ch of tch to join, turn—102 (118, 132, 148) dc.

RND 32: Ch 3 (counts as one dc), dc in ea dc around, sl st in 3rd ch of tch, turn.

Rep Rnd 32 four more times, fasten off, weave in ends.

G. SLEEVES

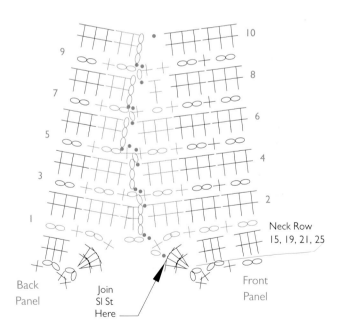

F. EDGING ROW

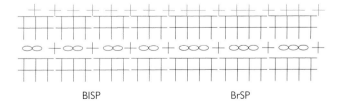

BISP   BrSP

Stitch Pattern Styles
117

Finishing

Lay jacket down flat to schematic measurements, pin in place. Using iron, steam block jacket to desired softness. Allow to dry.

Collar

With MC, ch 107 (107, 114, 114).

ROW 1 (RS): Dc in 4th ch from hook (tch counts as one dc), dc in ea remaining ch across, turn. Place stitch marker in 27th dc from ea end—105 (105, 112, 112) dc.

ROW 2: Ch 3 (counts as one dc throughout), dc in first dc (inc made), *dc in ea dc across to stitch marker, 2 dc in marked dc (move marker to first dc); repeat from * once (move marker to second dc), dc in ea dc across to last dc, 2 dc in last dc, turn—109 (109, 116, 116) dc.

Rep Row 2 three times—121 (121, 128, 128) dc.

ROW 6: Ch 2, dc in first dc (inc made), *dc in ea dc across to stitch marker, 2 dc in stitch marker dc; rep from * once, dc in ea dc across to last dc, (dc, hdc) in last dc, fasten off, weave in ends—123 (123, 130, 130) dc.

Join yarn with sl st and RS facing at foundation ch, sc evenly down collar diagonal edge (row edge), across Row 6, and up other diagonal edge, sl st to fasten off, weave in ends.

Line up center of collar with center back of neck, pin collar to neck with wrong sides facing. Using MC and large tapestry needle, whipstitch collar to neck. Fasten off, weave in ends.

Arm Band

(Make 2)

With CC, ch 6.

ROW 1: Sc in 2nd ch from hook, sc in ea remaining ch across, turn—5 sc.

ROW 2: Ch 1, sc in ea sc across, turn.

Rep Row 2 until the band measures 13 (14¼, 17, 19)" (33 [36, 43, 48.5] cm), turn.

RND 1 (RS): Ch 1, sc in ea sc across to last sc, 3 sc in last sc, turn 90 degrees, sc evenly along long edge (row edge) to opposite side, 3 sc in first ch of foundation row, sc in ea ch across to last ch, 3 sc in last ch, turn 90 degrees, sc evenly along long edge to first sc, 2 sc in same st as first sc, sl st in first sc to join, fasten off, weave in ends.

Overlay band ends 1" (2.5 cm), pin in place. Sew button to arm band with yarn and tapestry needle though both ends. Slip band onto sleeve just above ruffle. (Optional) With CC and tapestry needle, backstitch arm band to sleeve. Rep for second arm band.

Back Band

(Make 2)

With CC, ch 8.

ROW 1: Sc in 2nd ch from hook, sc in ea remaining ch across, turn—7 sc.

ROW 2: Ch 1, sc in ea sc across, turn.

Rep Row 2 sixteen more times.

ROW 19 (BUTTONHOLE ROW): Ch 1, sc in next 2 sc, ch 3, skip 3 sc, sc in last 2 sc, turn.

ROW 20: Ch 1, sc in next 2 sc, 3 sc in ch-3 sp, sc in last 2 sc, turn.

ROW 21: Ch 1, sc2tog over first 2 sc, sc in next 3 sc, sc2tog over last 2 sc, turn—5 sc.

ROW 22: Ch 1, sc2tog over first 2 sc, sc in next sc, sc2tog over last 2 sc, turn—3 sc.

RND 23 (RS): Ch 1, sc2tog over first 2 sc, 2 sc in last sc, turn 90 degrees, sc evenly along long edge to Row 1, 3 sc in first ch of foundation row, sc in ea ch across to last ch, 3 sc in last ch, turn 90 degrees, sc evenly along long edge to first sc2tog, sc in same st as sc2tog, sl st in first sc to join, fasten off, weave in ends.

Pin back band to back of the body at the waist, placing square edge under arm with tabbed edge pointing to center of back. Sew back band to back with CC and tapestry needle. Cut two 2 (5" cm) pieces of grosgrain ribbon. Fold edges down and pin to inside (WS) of back. Pin one piece at buttonhole opening with the waist laying flat. Pin the other piece 1½" (4 cm) toward center back from the first or at the buttonhole opening with the waist cinched to your preference. Sew ribbon to body with sewing needle and thread. Sew buttons to outside (RS) of back at ribbon locations with sewing needle and thread. Repeat for second back band on opposite side of back.

Cut remaining grosgrain ribbon into 2" (5 cm) pieces. Fold down edges of each piece of ribbon. Try jacket on. Overlap right front panel over left front panel. Lining up the outside corner edge of each panel with the neck edge, locate and pin one set of ribbon pieces to each side of the front panel where you would like the snap fasteners to close. Sew ribbons with needle and thread. Sew 3 pieces vertically to wrong side of right panel beg 2" (5 cm) from neck edge and spaced 2" (5 cm) apart. Sew remaining pieces to the inside side of the left front panel 2" (5 cm) from the neck edge and 2" (5 cm) apart. Sew snap fasteners and buttons to ribbon pieces through RS of fabric with matching thread and sewing needle. (Optional) Pin extra ribbon along neck edge, fold down edges. Sew in place with sewing thread and needle for extra stability at neck.

Rebecca Vest

After pouring through my old teen magazines from the early '80s with my niece, Rebecca, I had the strongest desire to create something from my teenage era. I was always drawn to the classic tennis outfit–clad models. Laughing at my funny whim, I thought, "How can I make a classic tennis jersey vest without throwing us too literally back into the '80s?" This vest, with its modern scoop neck, updated colors, and cute eyelets, is my version of a teenage infatuation, turned into flattering fashion.

Equipment

YARN: Fingering-weight (#1 Super Fine)

Shown: Lorna's Laces Shepard Sock (80% Superwash Wool, 20% Nylon; 215 yd [196.5 m]/2 oz [57 g]): pine (MC), 4 (5, 6, 7) hanks; natural (CC), 1 (1, 2, 2) hanks.

HOOK: F/5 (3.75 mm) or hook needed to obtain gauge.

NOTIONS: Tapestry needle; straight pins.

GAUGE: 22 st (1.5 SR) by 12 rows (1.5 RR) = 4 x 4″ (10 x 10 cm) in Eyelet Stitch Pattern.

SIZE: Small (Medium, Large, X-Large) fits 28 (34, 39, 45)″ (71 [86.5, 99, 114.5] cm) bust circumference.

Vest shown in size Medium.

NOTES: *The vest is crocheted in the round to the arm opening.*
It is then divided into the front and back and worked in rows to the seam at the shoulder.

The Plans

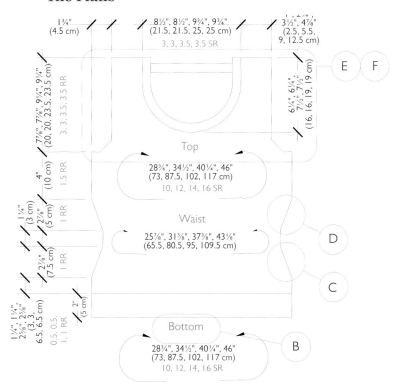

Special Stitch

This pattern is worked off of a base st, an alternative to other foundation stitches that will match the weight of the rest of the pattern, and reduce bulk, in addition to creating an attractive edge.

Base Stitch (base st)

Chain 3 (counts as one base st).

Set-up stitch: Yarn over hook, insert hook into the 3rd chain from hook (**Figure 1**), yarn over hook and draw up a loop (3 loops on hook), yarn over hook, draw through 2 loops (2 loops on hook; **Figure 2**), yarn over hook, draw through the remaining 2 loops on hook.

Next stitch: *Yarn over hook, insert hook into top horizontal bars of previous stitch (near first ch of beg ch-3), yarn over hook; (**Figure 3**) and draw up a loop (3 loops on hook), yarn over hook, draw through 2 loops, yarn over hook, draw through remaining 2 loops on hook (**Figure 4**). Repeat from * (this becomes the bottom edge of the base st; to work next row, flip work and continue according to patt).

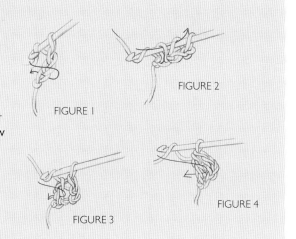

A. EYELET STITCH PATTERN (ESP)

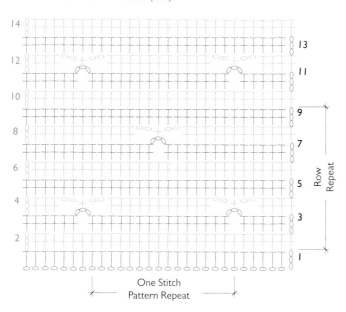

One Stitch
Pattern Repeat

Foundation

Eyelet Stitch Pattern (ESP)

See stitch diagram A for assistance.

ROW 1: Ch 3 (counts as first base st), 28 base st, turn—29 base st.

ROW 2: Ch 3 (counts as one dc thoughout), dc in ea st across, turn—29 dc.

ROW 3: Ch 3, dc in next 5 dc, *ch 3, skip one dc, dc in next 15 dc; rep from * across to last 7 dc, ch 3, skip one dc, dc in ea dc to end, turn.

ROW 4: Ch 3, dc in ea dc to 2 dc before ch-3 sp, *ch 2, skip 2 dc, sc in ch-3 sp, ch 2, skip 2 dc, dc in next 11 dc; rep from * across, end with ch 2, skip 2 dc, sc in ch-3 sp, ch 2, skip 2 dc, dc in ea dc to end, turn.

B. BOTTOM BODY

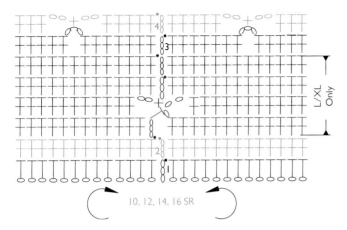

10, 12, 14, 16 SR

L/XL Only

ROW 5: Ch 3, dc in ea dc to ch-2 sp, *2 dc in ch-2 sp, dc in sc, 2 dc in ch-2 sp, dc in ea dc to next ch-2 sp; rep from * across, turn.

ROW 6: Rep Row 2.

ROW 7: Ch 3, dc in next 13 dc, *ch 3, skip one dc, dc in next 15 dc; rep from * across, ch 3, skip one dc, dc in ea dc to end, turn.

ROWS 8–9: Rep Rows 4–5.

Rep Rows 2–9 to desired length.

Construction

Body

RND 1 (RS): With MC, ch 3 (counts as a base st), base st 159 (191, 223, 255), sl st to 3rd ch of tch, turn—160, 192, 224, 256 fdc; 10, 12, 14, 16 SR.

Next RNDS: Cont with stitch diagram B, working in turned rnds of ESP.

C. WAIST SHAPING

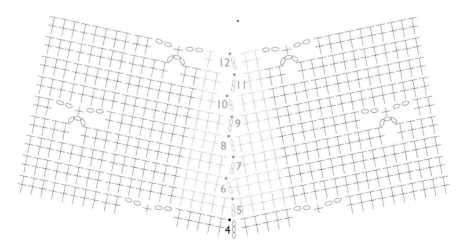

Waist Shaping

Note: Remove two sts ea rnd in this section. Remove one st ea side of waist. See stitch diagram C for assistance.

RND 5 (RS): Ch 2 (does not count as a dc throughout), cont in row 5 of ESP for 79 (95, 111, 127) dc (5 [6, 7, 8] SR), dc2tog over next 2 dc, cont in Row 5 of ESP around, sl st to first dc, turn—158 (190, 222, 254) dc.

RND 6: Ch 2, rep Row 2 of ESP to dc2tog, dc2tog over dc2tog and next dc, cont with Row 2 of ESP to end, sl st to first dc, turn—156 (188, 220, 252) dc.

RND 7: Ch 2, dc in next 14 dc, cont in Row 7 of ESP around to dc2tog, dc2tog over dc2tog and next dc, dc in next 13 dc, cont in Row 7 of ESP to end, sl st to first dc, turn.

RND 8: Ch 2, cont in Row 8 of ESP around to dc2tog, dc2tog over dc2tog and next dc, dc in next 12 dc, cont in Row 8 of ESP to end, sl st to first dc, turn.

RND 9: Ch 2, cont in Row 5 of ESP around to dc2tog, dc2tog over dc2tog and next dc, cont in Row 5 of ESP to end, sl st to first dc, turn—150 (182, 214, 246) dc.

RND 10: Rep Rnd 6—148 (180, 212, 244) dc.

RND 11: Ch 2, dc in next 4 dc, cont in Row 3 of ESP around, dc2tog over dc2tog and next dc, dc in next 3 dc, cont in Row 3 of ESP to end, sl st to first dc, turn.

RND 12: Ch 2, cont in Row 4 of ESP around to dc2tog, dc2tog over dc2tog and next dc, dc in next dc, cont in Row 4 of ESP to end, sl st to first dc, turn.

Waist

RND 1 (RS): Ch 3, cont in Row 5 of ESP around, sl st to 3rd ch of tch, turn—144 (176, 208, 240) dc.

RND 2: Rep Row 2 of ESP around, sl st to 3rd ch of tch, turn.

RND 3: Ch 3, dc in next 11 dc, [ch 3, skip one dc, dc in next 15 dc] 3 (4, 5, 6) times, ch 3, skip one dc, dc in next 23 dc, *ch 3, skip one dc, dc in next 15 dc; rep from * across to end, sl st to 3rd ch of tch, turn.

RND 4: Ch 3, dc in ea dc to last 2 dc before ch-3 sp, *ch 2, skip 2 dc, sc in ch-3 sp, ch 2, skip 2 dc, dc in next dc, dc in ea dc to last 2 dc before next ch-3 sp; rep from * across, sl st to 3rd ch of tch, turn.

RND 3: Ch 3, dc in sl st, dc in next 4 dc, cont in Row 3 of ESP around to inc, dc in 1st dc of inc, 2 dc in 2nd dc of inc, dc in next 4 dc, cont in Row 3 of ESP, sl st to 3rd ch of tch, turn.

RND 4: Ch 3, dc in sl st, cont in Row 4 of ESP around to inc, dc in 1st dc of inc, 2 dc in 2nd dc of inc, cont in Row 4 of ESP, sl st to 3rd ch of tch, turn.

RND 5: Ch 3, dc in sl st, cont in Row 5 of ESP around to inc, dc in 1st dc of inc, 2 dc in 2nd dc of inc, cont in Row 5 of ESP, sl st to 3rd ch of tch, turn—154 (186, 218, 250) dc.

RND 6: Rep Rnd 2 of bust shaping—156 (188, 220, 252) dc.

RND 7: Ch 3, dc in sl st, dc in next 14 dc, cont in Row 7 of ESP around to inc, dc in 1st dc of inc, 2 dc in 2nd dc of inc, dc in next 14 dc, cont in Row 7 of ESP, sl st to 3rd ch of tch, turn.

RND 8: Ch 3, dc in sl st, dc in next 4 dc, cont in Row 8 of ESP around to inc, dc in 1st dc of inc, 2 dc in 2nd dc of inc, dc in next 4 dc, cont in Row 8 of ESP, sl st to 3rd ch of tch, turn.

Bust

RNDS 1–2: Follow Rows 9 and 2 of ESP, sl st to 3rd ch of tch, turn—160 (192, 224, 256) dc; 10 (12, 14, 16) SR.

RND 3 (RS): Ch 3, dc in next 6 dc, cont in Row 3 of ESP around, sl st to 3rd ch of tch, turn.

RND 4: Ch 3, cont in Row 4 of ESP around, sl st to 3rd ch of tch, turn.

RNDS 5–6: Follow Rows 5 and 2 of ESP, sl st to 3rd ch of tch, turn.

RND 7: Ch 3, dc in next 14 dc, cont in Row 7 of ESP to last dc, ch 1, hdc to 3rd ch of tch, turn.

RND 8: Ch 2, skip 2 dc, cont in Row 8 of ESP to last 2 dc, ch 2, sc in hdc, turn.

Rep Rnds 1–4 of bust once more. Fasten off, weave in ends.

Bust Shaping

See stitch diagram D for assistance.

(Add two sts ea rnd in this section. Add one st ea side of waist.)

RND 1 (RS): Ch 3, dc in sl st, cont in Row 5 of ESP for 70 (86, 102, 118) dc, 2 dc in next dc (inc made), cont in Row 5 of ESP, sl st to 3rd ch of tch, turn—146 (178, 210, 242) dc.

RND 2: Ch 3, dc in sl st, cont in Row 2 of ESP around to inc, dc in 1st dc of inc, 2 dc in 2nd dc of inc, cont in Row 2 of ESP, sl st to 3rd ch of tch, turn—148 (180, 212, 244) dc.

D. BUST SHAPING

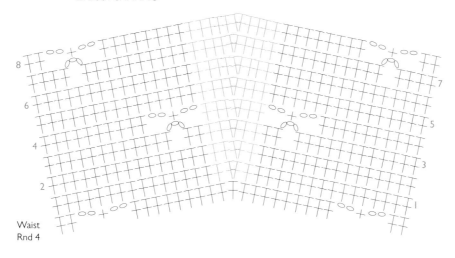

8
6
4
2

Waist
Rnd 4

7
5
3
1

E. BACK PANEL

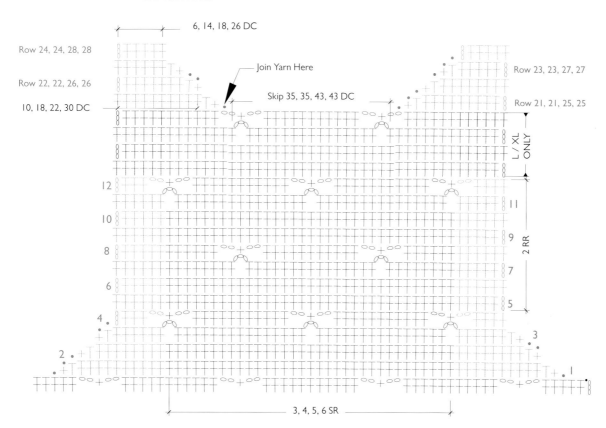

6, 14, 18, 26 DC

Row 24, 24, 28, 28

Row 22, 22, 26, 26

10, 18, 22, 30 DC

Join Yarn Here

Skip 35, 35, 43, 43 DC

Row 23, 23, 27, 27

Row 21, 21, 25, 25

L / XL
ONLY

12
10
8
6
4
2

11
9
7
5
3
1

2 RR

3, 4, 5, 6 SR

F. FRONT PANEL

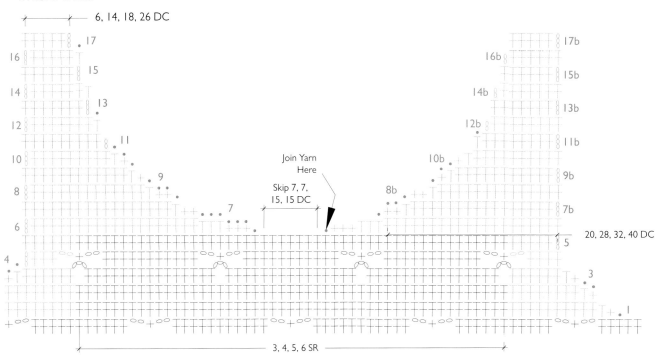

6, 14, 18, 26 DC

20, 28, 32, 40 DC

Join Yarn Here

Skip 7, 7, 15, 15 DC

3, 4, 5, 6 SR

Back Panel

Work will now be divided into a front and back and worked in rows.

With RS facing, skip 2 dc from where you fastened off with sl st, join yarn with sl st to next st.

Beg with Row 1, follow stitch diagram E.

Right Shoulder Shaping

ROW 21 (21, 25, 25) (RS): Ch 3, dc in next 9 (17, 21, 29) st, hdc in next st, sc in next st, sl st in next st, leave rem sts unworked, turn.

Cont with stitch diagram E to end, fasten off. Join yarn with sl st in st indicated and cont with stitch diagram E for left shoulder shaping.

Front Panel

ARM OPENING

With RS of front facing, join yarn with sl st 5 sts from last sl st on Row 1 of back.

Beg with Row 1, follow Stitch Diagram F.

RIGHT NECK SHAPING

ROW 6 (WS): Ch 3, dc in next 19 (27, 31, 39) dc, hdc in next 3 dc, sc in next 3 dc, sl st in next st, leave rem sts unworked, turn—20 (28, 32, 40) dc.

Cont with stitch diagram F. Even though stitch diagram does not show eyelets, cont with eyelets in stitch pattern until there are too few sts left on row.

ROW 18: Ch 3, dc in ea dc across, turn.

Rep Row 18 six (six, ten, ten) times, fasten off, weave in ends.

LEFT ARM AND SHOULDER SHAPING

ROW 6B: With WS facing, skip 7 (7, 15, 15) sts, join yarn with sl st in next st, sc in next 3 st, hdc in next 3 st, dc in ea dc across, turn—20 (28, 32, 40) dc.

Cont with stitch diagram F, working in ESP until there are too few sts left on row.

ROW 18B: Ch 3, dc in ea dc across, turn.

Rep Row 18b 6 (6, 10, 10) times, fasten off, weave in ends.

Finishing

Pin vest to schematic size. Steam with iron and allow to dry. With RS facing, sl st thru both front and back evenly along shoulder seam. Turn top right side out. Join MC yarn with sl st to arm opening with right side facing, ch 1, sc evenly around arm opening, sl st to first sc. Fasten off and weave in ends.

Neck Collar

Join CC yarn with sl st to right side of neck opening, ch 7.

ROW 1: Sc in 2nd ch from hook and ea ch across, sl st to neck edge twice (first sl st joins collar to body, second sl st counts as tch), turn—6 sc.

ROW 2: Skip both sl st, sc-blp in ea sc across, turn.

ROW 3: Ch 1, sc-blp in ea sc across, sl st to neck edge twice, turn.

Rep Rows 2–3 evenly around neck opening, fasten off, weave in ends.

Body Ribbing

Join CC yarn with sl st to right side of bottom edge at seam, ch 13.

ROW 1: Sc in 2nd ch from hook and ea ch across, sl st to sleeve edge twice (first sl st joins ribbing to body, second sl st counts as tch), turn—12 sc.

Rep Rows 2–3 as for neck collar evenly around body opening. Fasten off, weave in ends.

Whipstitch ribbing seams together.

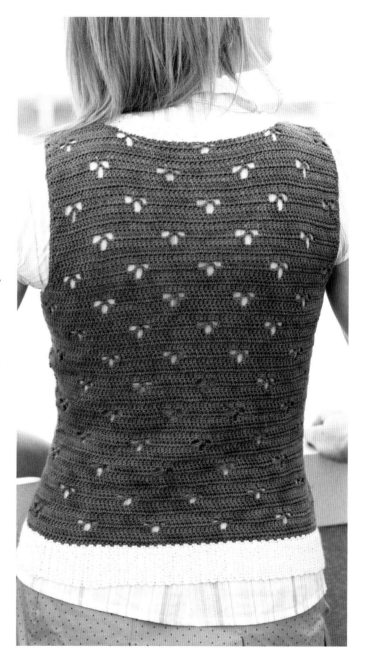

Christin Crop

With all the sweaters this season going long and baggy, I knew I would have to come up with something special to be able to pull off this style without looking like I was wearing a muumuu. My natural instinct was to design something with a cropped length to define my waist. After watching my older niece try to wear her little sister Christin's jacket, a lightbulb went on. I needed a cropped and fitted sweater to show off my figure while revealing a long, loose tunic underneath.

Equipment

YARN: Worsted-weight (#4 Medium)

Shown: Lorna's Laces Lion and Lamb (50% Silk, 50% Wool; 205 yd [187.5 m]/ 3.5 oz [100 g]): #6ns douglas fir, 4 (5, 6, 7) hanks.

HOOK: H/8 (5 mm) or hook needed to obtain gauge.

NOTIONS: Tapestry needle; three hook and eye closures; 12″ (30.5 cm) of ¾″ (2 cm)-wide grosgrain ribbon; matching sewing thread and needle; two 1 ½″ (4 cm) shank buttons; straight pins.

GAUGE: 21 sts (7 SR) by 12 rows (6 RR) = 4⅛″ x 4″ (10.5 x 10 cm) in stitch pattern.

SIZE: Small (Medium, Large, X-Large) fits 32 (36, 42, 46)″ (81.5 [91.5, 107, 117] cm) bust circumference.

Top shown in size Small.

The Plans

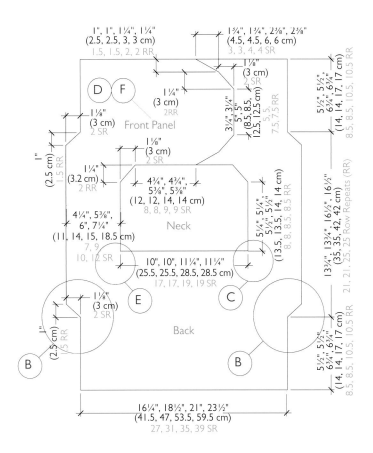

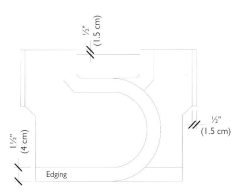

Edging

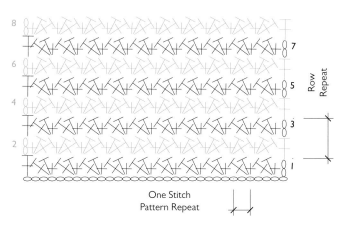

One Stitch
Pattern Repeat

Foundation

Crunch Shell Stitch Pattern (CSSP)

See stitch diagram A for assistance. Ch 34.

ROW 1: (Sc, hdc, dc) in 4th ch from hook, *skip next 2 ch, (sc, hdc, dc) in next ch; rep from * to last 3 ch, skip 2 ch, dc in last ch, turn—31 st, 10 SR.

ROW 2: Ch 2, skip first dc, *(sc, hdc, dc) in next dc, skip hdc, sc; rep from * to end, dc in tch, turn.

Rep Row 2 to desired length.

Construction

Back

Ch 85, 97, 109, 121.

ROW 1 (RS): Follow Row 1 of CSSP—82 (94, 106, 118) st; 27 (31, 35, 39) SR.

Repeat Row 2 of CSSP 16 (16, 20, 20) times—8 (8, 10, 10) RR.

Arm Shaping

See stitch diagram B for assistance with arm shaping.

ROW 1: Follow Row 2 of CSSP to end, (sc, hdc, 2 dc) in top of tch, turn—85 (97, 109, 121) st; 28 (32, 36, 40) SR.

ROW 2: Ch 4, cont in Row 2 of CSSP across, end with (sc, hdc, 2 dc) in top of tch, turn—88 (100, 112, 124) st; 29 (33, 37, 41) SR.

Rep Row 2 once and then rep Row 1 once—94 (106, 118, 130) st; 31 (35, 39, 43) SR.

Rep Row 2 of CSSP 11 (11, 15, 15) more times—7.5 (7.5, 9.5, 9.5) RR from beg of arm shaping.

B. ARM INCREASE

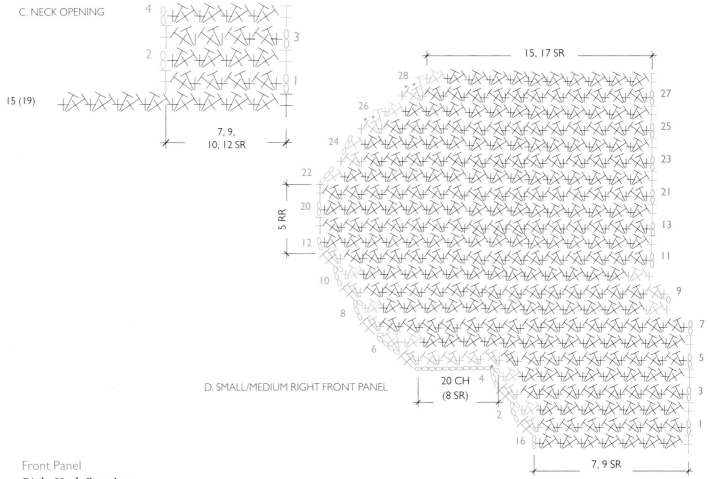

C. NECK OPENING

15 (19)

7, 9, 10, 12 SR

5 RR

15, 17 SR

D. SMALL/MEDIUM RIGHT FRONT PANEL

20 CH (8 SR)

7, 9 SR

Front Panel

Right Neck Opening

See diagram C for assistance with right neck opening.

ROW 1: Follow Row 2 of CSSP for 21 (27, 30, 36) st, skip next (hdc, sc), dc in next dc, leave rem sts unworked, turn—7 (9, 10, 12) SR.

Rep Row 2 of CSSP 15 times—8 RR from beg of neck opening.

L, XL Only: Rep Row 2 of CSSP once more.

Neck and Body Shaping

Follow stitch diagram D (Small/Medium or Large/X-Large) beg with Row 1. Fasten off, weave in ends.

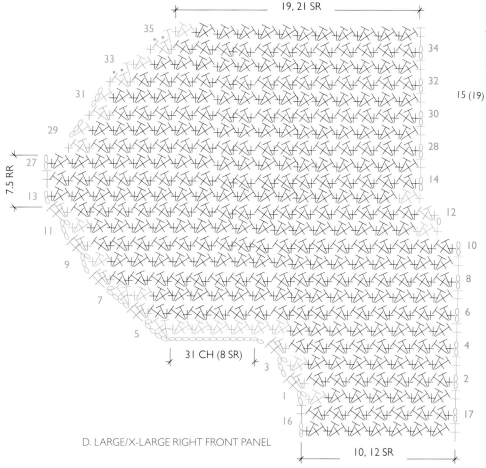

19, 21 SR

35
33
31
29
27
7.5 RR
13
11
9
7
5
3
1
16

34
32
30
28
14
12
10
8
6
4
2
17

31 CH (8 SR)

10, 12 SR

D. LARGE/X-LARGE RIGHT FRONT PANEL

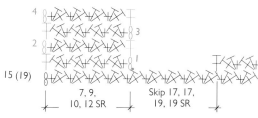

4
2
15 (19)

3
1

7, 9,
10, 12 SR

Skip 17, 17,
19, 19 SR

E. LEFT SIDE NECK OPENING

F. LEFT SMALL/MEDIUM FRONT PANEL

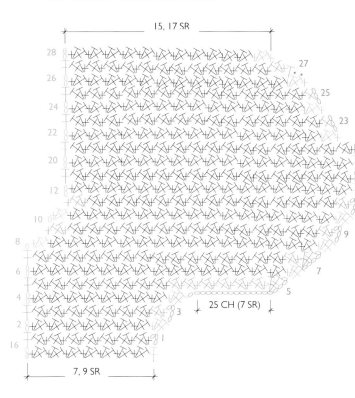

Finishing

Pin jacket to schematic size. Spritz with water, and allow to dry. With RS facing, whipstitch side seams together with yarn and large needle, fasten off, weave in ends. Turn right side out.

Arm Cuff

With RS facing, join yarn with sl st to the underside of the arm sleeve seam.

RND 1: Ch 1, sc evenly around arm opening, sl st to first sc, turn.

RNDS 2–3: Ch 1, sc in ea sc around, sl st to first sc, turn.

Fasten off, weave in ends.

F. LEFT LARGE/X-LARGE FRONT PANEL

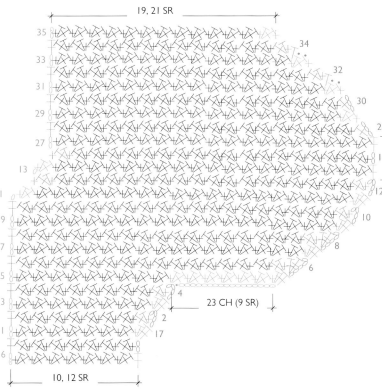

Left Front Panel

See diagram E for left side neck opening. See diagram F (Small/Medium or Large/X-Large) for assistance with left front panel.

ROW 1: Skip 16 (16, 18, 18) SR from last dc on opposite neck, join yarn to next hdc with sl st, ch 2, skip next sc, (sc, hdc, dc) in next dc, cont in Row 2 of CSSP across, turn—7 (9, 10, 12) SR.

Rep Row 2 of CSSP 15 times—8 RR from beg of neck opening.

L, XL Only: Rep Row 2 of CSSP once more.

Cont with stitch diagram E. Fasten off, weave in ends.

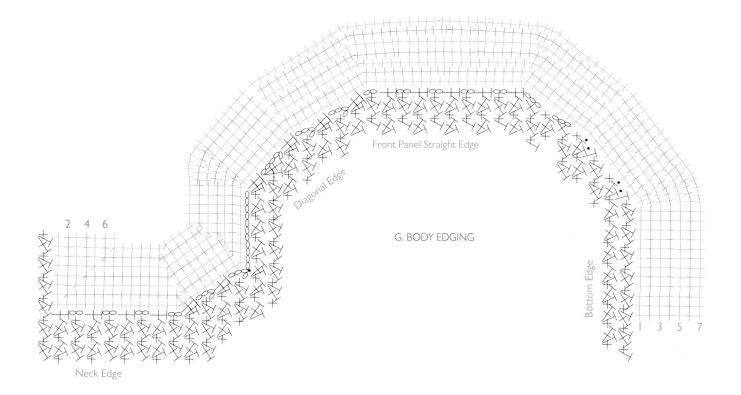

2 4 6

Neck Edge

Diagonal Edge

Front Panel Straight Edge

G. BODY EDGING

Bottom Edge

1 3 5 7

Body Edging

See stitch diagram G for assistance with edging.

With right side facing, join yarn with sl st to the side seam of the body.

RND 1: Ch 1, sc evenly around body opening, sl st to first sc, turn.

RND 2: Ch 1, sc in ea sc along bottom edge, neck edge, and diagonal front edges, sc3tog in all neck corners, sc2tog in inside corners of neck to panel, 2 sc in outside corners of panel to bottom and diagonal to straight edges, 2 sc in middle of front straight edge, sl st to first sc, turn.

RND 3: Ch 1, sc in ea sc along all edges, sc3tog in inside corners, sc2tog in inside corners of neck to panel, 2 sc in outside corners of panel to bottom and diagonal to straight edges, sl st to first sc, turn.

RND 4: Ch 1, sc in ea sc around working sc3tog in each of the back neck corners, sc2tog in each inside corner where shoulder meets the front right and left panels, 2 sc in outside corners

of panel to bottom and diagonal to straight edges, 2 sc in third points of front straight edge, sl st to first sc, turn.

RND 5: Rep Rnd 3.

RND 6: Rep Rnd 2.

RND 7: Rep Rnd 3, fasten off, weave in ends.

Cut grosgrain ribbon into six 2" (5 cm) pieces. Fold down edges of each piece of ribbon. With matching thread and sewing needle, sew 2 ribbon pieces to back side of edging on front right panel where you would like the fasteners to close. Sew one piece to inside of same panel across from where opposite panel will connect at neck edge about 2" (5 cm) in from front neck edge. Sew remaining pieces to outside of left front panel, matching ribbon placement on the right side. Sew hook and eye closures to ribbon pieces with matching thread and sewing needle. Sew buttons to outside of right panel along the edge with yarn and large needle.

Courtney Corset Top

Every little sister dreams of having a big sister like mine. Courtney is one of those sisters that is so cool, yet always happy to bring you along to any event, and make you feel like part of the gang. This top reminds me of her, very fashionable but still casual enough to pair with your most relaxed jeans. Mixing feminine lacy stitches with a solid corset gives the top a flirty quality along with a fitted shape that will accentuate your figure.

Equipment

YARN: Fingering-weight (#1 Super Fine)

Shown: Blue Sky Alpaca Royal (100% Alpaca; 288 yd [263.5 m]/ 3.5 oz. [100 g]):

#702 spanish leather, 4 (4, 5, 6) hanks.

HOOK: F/5 (3.75 mm) or hook size needed to obtain gauge.

NOTIONS: Tapestry needle; straight pins.

GAUGE: 24 sts (2 SR) by 12 rows (6 RR) = 4 x 4¼″ (10 x 11 cm) in Fairy Wing Stitch Pattern; 20 sts = 4″ (10 cm) in Ribbing Pattern.

SIZE: Small (Medium, Large, X-Large) fits 32 (36, 40, 44)″ (81.5 [91.5, 101.5, 112] cm) bust circumference.

Top shown in size Small.

The Plans

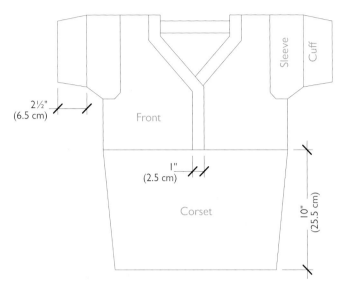

2½"
(6.5 cm)

Front

1"
(2.5 cm)

Corset

10"
(25.5 cm)

Sleeve

Cuff

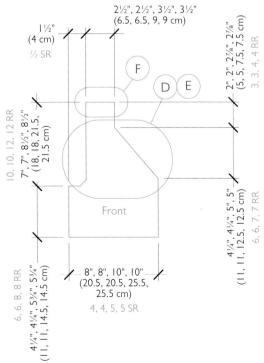

1½"
(4 cm)
½ SR

2½", 2½", 3½", 3½"
(6.5, 6.5, 9, 9 cm)

F

D E

2", 2", 2⅞", 2⅞"
(5, 5, 7.5, 7.5 cm)
3, 3, 4, 4 RR

10, 10, 12, 12 RR

7", 7", 8½", 8½"
(18, 18, 21.5,
21.5 cm)

Front

4¼", 4¼", 5", 5"
(11, 11, 12.5, 12.5 cm)
6, 6, 7, 7 RR

6, 6, 8, 8 RR

4¼", 4¼", 5¾", 5¾"
(11, 11, 14.5, 14.5 cm)

8", 8", 10", 10"
(20.5, 20.5, 25.5,
25.5 cm)
4, 4, 5, 5 SR

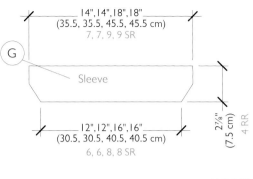

14", 14", 18", 18"
(35.5, 35.5, 45.5, 45.5 cm)
7, 7, 9, 9 SR

G

Sleeve

12", 12", 16", 16"
(30.5, 30.5, 40.5, 40.5 cm)
6, 6, 8, 8 SR

2⅞"
(7.5 cm)
4 RR

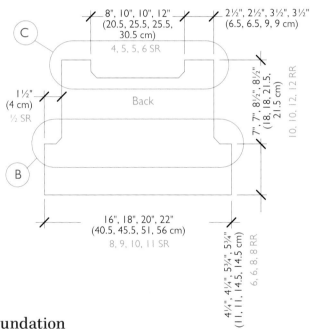

8", 10", 10", 12"
(20.5, 25.5, 25.5,
30.5 cm)
4, 5, 5, 6 SR

2½", 2½", 3½", 3½"
(6.5, 6.5, 9, 9 cm)

C

1½"
(4 cm)
½ SR

Back

7", 7", 8½", 8½"
(18, 18, 21.5,
21.5 cm)
10, 10, 12, 12 RR

B

16", 18", 20", 22"
(40.5, 45.5, 51, 56 cm)
8, 9, 10, 11 SR

4¼", 4¼", 5¾", 5¾"
(11, 11, 14.5, 14.5 cm)
6, 6, 8, 8 RR

Foundation

Fairy Wing Stitch Pattern

See stitch diagram A for assistance. Ch 40.

ROW 1: Sc in 2nd ch from hook, *ch 2, skip one ch, sc in next ch, skip 3 ch, (3 tr, ch 4, sc) in next ch, ch 2, skip one ch, (sc, ch 4, 3 tr) in next ch, skip 3 ch, sc in next ch; rep from * to last 2 ch, ch 2, skip one ch, sc in last ch, turn—18 tr; 3 SR.

ROW 2: Ch 4 (counts as one dc and ch 1), dc in first ch-2 sp, *ch 1, skip 3 tr, sc in ch-4 sp, ch 2, dc2tog in ch-2 sp, ch 2, sc in ch-4 sp, ch 1, skip 3 tr, (dc, ch 1, dc) in ch-2 sp; rep from * to end, turn.

A. FAIRY WING STITCH PATTERN

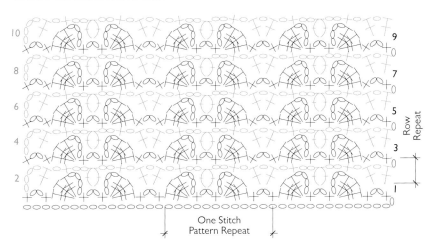

One Stitch Pattern Repeat

B. BACK ARM OPENING

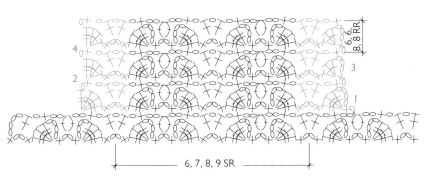

6, 7, 8, 9 SR

ROW 3: Ch 1, sc in dc, ch 2, skip first ch-1 sp, skip dc, *sc in next ch-1 sp, skip sc, (3 tr, ch 4, sc) in ch-2 sp, ch 2, skip dc2tog, (sc, ch 4, 3 tr) in ch-2 sp, skip sc, sc in ch-1 sp, ch 2, skip (dc, ch 1, dc); rep from * across, sc in last dc, turn—18 tr; 3 SR.
Rep Rows 2–3 to desired length.

Ribbing Pattern (rib patt)

ROW 1: Sc in 2nd ch from hook and ea ch across, sl st to edge twice (first sl st joins ribbing to front panel, second sl st counts as a turning ch), turn.

ROW 2: Skip both sl st, sc-flp in ea sc across, turn.

ROW 3: Ch 1, sc-blp in ea sc across, sl st to edge twice, turn.
Rep Rows 2–3 for pattern.

Construction

Back

Ch 100 (112, 124, 136).

ROW 1 (RS): Follow Row 1 of Fairy Wing stitch pattern—48 (54, 60, 66) tr; 8 (9, 10, 11) SR.

Rep Rows 2–3 of Fairy Wing stitch pattern 5 (5, 7, 7) times—6 (6, 8, 8) RR.

Rep Row 2 once more before continuing, fasten off, weave in ends.

Arm Opening

With RS facing, skip (dc, ch 1, dc, ch 1, sc, ch 2, dc2tog), join yarn with sl st to next ch-2 sp, follow stitch diagram B for arm opening for 16 (16, 20, 20) rows.

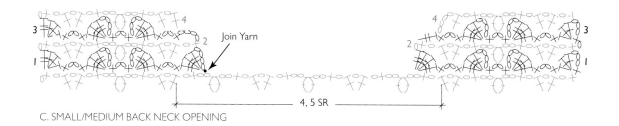

C. SMALL/MEDIUM BACK NECK OPENING

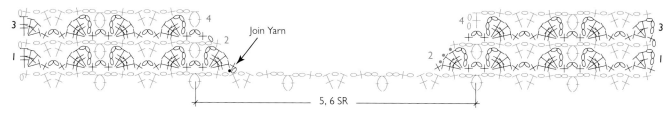

C. LARGE/X-LARGE BACK NECK OPENING

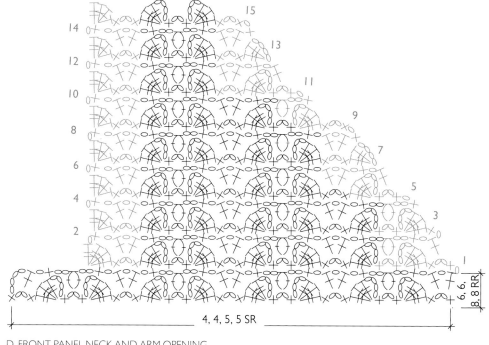

D. FRONT PANEL NECK AND ARM OPENING

Neck Opening

Follow stitch diagram C (Small/Medium or Large/X-Large) for neck opening and shoulders. Fasten off, weave in ends.

Front Panel

(Make 2)

Ch 52 (52, 64, 64).

ROW 1 (RS): Follow Row 1 of Fairy Wing stitch pattern—24 (24, 30, 30) tr; 4 (4, 5, 5) SR.

Rep Rows 2–3 of Fairy Wing stitch pattern 5 (5, 7, 7) times—6 (6, 8, 8) RR.

Rep Row 2 once more before continuing.

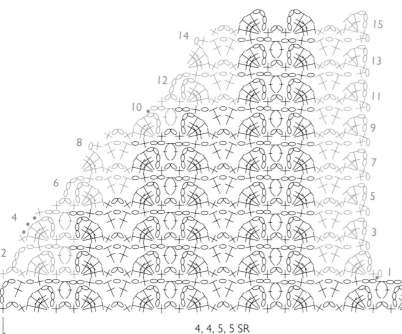

E. OPPOSITE FRONT PANEL NECK AND ARM OPENING

F. FRONT PANEL NECK AND SHOULDERS

Small and Medium

Large and X-large

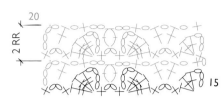

Opposite Front Panel S/M

Opposite Front Panel L/XL

G. SLEEVES

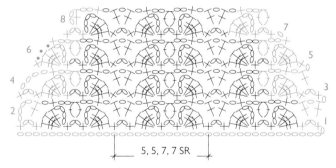

5, 5, 7, 7 SR

Arm Opening
Follow neck and arm opening stitch diagram D for front panel (p.142) and opposite front panel diagram F (above) for 15 rows.

Neck Opening
Follow front panel neck and shoulders stitch diagram F.

Sleeve

(Make 2)
Ch 88 (88, 112, 112).
Follow sleeve stitch diagram G. Fasten off, weave in ends.

Finishing

Pin panels to schematic size. Spritz with water, and allow to dry.
With RS facing, whipstitch shoulder seams and side seams of back
and front panels together. With RS facing, begin to pin sleeve to
arm opening by pinning bottom seams in place first and working extra fabric up toward shoulder; Sleeve sets 1½" (4 cm) into
panels. Evenly gather fabric at top shoulder; this will give a puffy
sleeve effect. Join yarn to bottom of sleeve seam, working thru
both pieces of fabric, sl st evenly along arm opening. Fasten off
and weave in ends. Whipstitch sleeve seam closed. Turn top
right side out.

Collar

With RS facing, join yarn with sl st to front panel bottom edge
neck opening, ch 6. Beg with Row 1, work in rib patt evenly
around neck opening, fasten off, weave in ends. (Optional)
Pin collar down and spritz with water. This stops the collar
from curling.

Cuff

With RS facing, join yarn with sl st to sleeve edge at seam, ch 13.
Beg with Row 1, work in rib patt evenly around sleeve opening,
fasten off, weave in ends. With RS facing, whipstitch cuff seams
together. (Optional) Pin cuff down and spritz with water.

Corset

Lay collar front edges on top of each other and pin in place.
Work corset through both fabrics at collar. With RS facing, join
yarn with sl st to body edge at side seam, ch 51. Beg with Row 1,
work in rib patt evenly around body opening, fasten off, weave
in ends. With RS facing, whipstitch corset seams together.
(Optional) Block corset by pinning down and spritzing with water.

Glossary

Abbreviations

bet	between		mc	main color
blp	backloop(s)		pm	place marker
bo	bobble		rep	repeat
cc	contrasting color		rnd	round
ch	chain		RR	row repeat
ch-sp	chain space		RS	right side
cm	centimeter		sc	single crochet
cont	continue		scxtog	single crochet x stitches together
dc	double crochet		sk	skip
dc-cl	double crochet cluster		sl st	slip stitch
dcxtog	double crochet x stitches together		sp	stitch pattern
dec	decrease		SR	stitch pattern repeat
dtr	double treble		st	stitch
est	establish		tch	turning chain
flp	front loop(s)		tog	together
fol	follow		tr	treble crochet
g	grams		WS	wrong side
hdc	half double crochet		yd	yard
inc	increase		yo	yarn over hook
lp	loop			
m	meter			

Techniques

Chain (ch)

Make a slipknot on hook. Yarn over hook and draw it through loop of slipknot. Repeat, drawing yarn through the last loop formed.

Single Crochet (sc)

Insert hook into a stitch, yarn over hook and draw up a loop (**Figure 1**), yarn over hook and draw it through both loops on hook (**Figure 2**).

FIGURE 1   FIGURE 2

Single Crochet 2 Together (sc2tog)

Insert hook into next stitch, yarn over hook, draw up loop (2 loops on hook; Insert hook into next stitch, yarn over, draw loop through stitch (3 loops on hook). Yarn over and draw yarn through all 3 loops on hook (**Figure 1**). Completed sc2tog— 1 stitch decreased (**Figure 2**).

In order to single crochet more stitches together, repeat above instructions to draw up loops the desired number of times before drawing yarn through all loops on hook.

FIGURE 1   FIGURE 2

Slip Stitch (sl st)

*Insert hook into stitch, yarn over hook and draw loop through stitch and loop on hook. Repeat from *.

Half Double Crochet (hdc)

*Yarn over hook, insert hook into a stitch, yarn over hook and draw up a loop (3 loops on hook), yarn over hook (**Figure 1**) and draw it through all the loops on the hook (**Figure 2**). Repeat from *.

FIGURE 1

FIGURE 2

Double Crochet (dc)

*Yarn over hook, insert hook into a stitch, yarn over hook and draw up a loop (3 loops on hook; **Figure 1**), yarn over hook and draw it through 2 loops (**Figure 2**), yarn over hook and draw it through the remaining 2 loops (**Figure 3**). Repeat from *.

FIGURE 1

FIGURE 2

FIGURE 3

Double Crochet Cluster (dc-cl)

Yarn over hook, [insert hook into st, yarn over hook, draw up loop, yarn over hook, draw through 2 loops on hook] 3 times, yarn over hook, draw through remaining 4 loops on hook (**Figure 1**).

FIGURE 1

Double Crochet 2 Together (dc2tog)

Yarn over hook, insert hook into next indicated stitch, yarn over hook and draw up a loop (**Figure 1**), yarn over hook and draw yarn through 2 loops, yarn over hook, insert hook into next indicated stitch and draw up a loop (4 loops on hook), yarn over hook, draw yarn through 2 loops (**Figure 2**), yarn over hook and draw yarn through the remaining 3 loops on hook (**Figure 3**). Completed dc2tog—1 stitch decreased (**Figure 4**) or one cluster with 2 sts together.

In order to double crochet more stitches together, complete through Figure 2 above the same number of times as the number of stitches you wish to crochet together, then draw yarn through all remaining loops on hook.

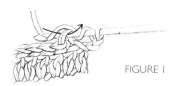

FIGURE 1

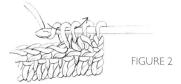

FIGURE 2

FIGURE 3

FIGURE 4

Treble Crochet (tr)

*Wrap yarn around hook 2 times, insert hook into stitch, yarn over hook and draw up a loop (4 loops on hook; **Figure 1**), yarn over hook and draw it through 2 loops (**Figure 2**), yarn over hook and draw it through the next 2 loops, yarn over hook and draw it through the remaining 2 loops (**Figure 3**). Repeat from *.

FIGURE 1

FIGURE 2

FIGURE 3

Double Treble Crochet (dtr)

*Wrap yarn around hook 3 times, insert hook into stitch, yarn over hook and draw up a loop (5 loops on hook), [yarn over hook and draw it through 2 loops] 4 times. Repeat from *.

Resources

The yarns used in the book were all donated graciously by the yarn companies.
Thank you so much for all your support and quick response to all my requests.
I truly appreciate all that you have given me.

Yarn Companies

Blue Sky Alpacas
PO Box 88
Cedar, MN 55011
(888) 460-8862
blueskyalpacas.com
Blue Sky Cotton
Alpaca Sportweight
Royal

Coats and Clark
PO Box 12229
Greenville, SC 29612
(800) 648-1479
coatsandclark.com
Aunt Lydia's Classic
  Crochet Thread
Aunt Lydia's Fashion
  Crochet Thread
Aunt Lydia's Cable
  Crochet Thread

Lily Chin Signature Collection
5333 Casgrain #1204
Montreal, QC H2T 1X3
Canada
(877) 244-1204
lilychinsignaturecollection.com
Chelsea

Lorna's Laces
4229 North Honore Street
Chicago, IL 60613
(773) 935-3803
lornaslaces.net
Swirl DK
Shepard Sock
Lion and Lamb

Louet
3425 Hands Road
Prescott, ON
Canada
(613) 925-4502
louet.com
Euroflax Sportweight
Merlin Sportweight
Gems Sportweight

South West Trading Company
(866) 794-1818
soysilk.com
Vickie Howell Signature
  Collection Rock
Vickie Howell Signature
  Collection Love
Oasis
Bamboo

Beads and Findings

Bass Pro Shops
800 BASS-PRO
www.basspro.com
Fireline

Beadalon
440 Highlands Boulevard
Coatesville, PA 19320
(866) 423-2325
beadalon.com
Crimp beads

Michael's
michaels.com
beads

Sulky
980 Cobb Place Boulevard
Suite 130
Kennesaw, GA 30144
(800) 874-4115
sulky.com
Invisible thread

Westrim Crafts
Creativity Inc.
7855 Hayvenhurst Avenue
Van Nuys, CA 91406
(800) 727-2727
westrimcrafts.com
Toggle clasp, seed beads, glass
beads, silver purse hoops

Index

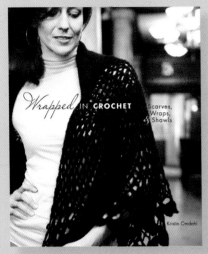

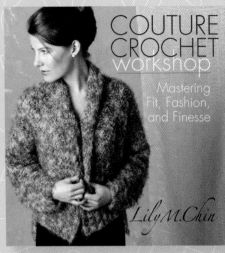